# Developing Strengths-Based Project Teams

# Developing Strengths-Based Project Teams

Martha Buelt, MA and Connie Plowman, PMP®

BUSINESS EXPERT PRESS

*Developing Strengths-Based Project Teams*

First published in 2018 by
Business Expert Press, LLC
222 East 46th Street, New York, NY 10017
www.businessexpertpress.com

ISBN-13: 978-1-94784-341-7 (paperback)
ISBN-13: 978-1-94784-342-4 (e-book)

Business Expert Press Portfolio and Project Management Collection

Collection ISSN: 2156-8189 (print)
Collection ISSN: 2156-8200 (electronic)

Cover and interior design by Exeter Premedia Services Private Ltd., Chennai, India

First edition: 2018

10 9 8 7 6 5 4 3 2 1

Printed in the United States of America.

# Disclaimers

# Abstract

Everyone has talents and strengths. Everyone does projects. *Developing Strengths-Based Project Teams* integrates common project management and strengths-based talent development language to help you and your project team learn about and become a strengths-based project team.

This book is designed for project managers, team members, and stakeholders who have an interest in talent development—not only their own talents and strengths, but also the combined talents and strengths of their project teams. Strengths-based project teams integrate their knowledge, skills, and practice of strengths development with project management tools and techniques, equipping the project team to apply and maximize their collective strengths to successfully complete their project on time, within budget, and according to the project objectives and specifications.

The authors provide a series of building blocks (i.e., discovering, appreciating, and articulating, plus applying talents, knowledge, skills, experience, and strengths) for individual strengths development. This is followed by cultivating the collective strengths of the project team members to become a strengths-based project team.

Throughout the book, there are exercises, templates, and action plans to guide you, along with reflective questions. You will learn the characteristics of a strengths-based project team and explore the various project management roles—including the project sponsor and functional managers—for sustaining a strengths-based project team culture.

A strengths-based project team culture creates an environment in which team members can use their talent development tools long-term to develop and apply what they naturally do best, resulting in higher project team performance.

# Keywords

coaching, functional manager, mentoring, project management, project management (PM) tool kit, project manager, project sponsor, project team, stakeholder, strengths-based project team, talent development, team development, team member

# Contents

# Preface

Our story. Putting together a high-performing, strengths-based project team can be easily done—like ours! Take the two authors. One is named Martha. The other is Connie. Martha lives in Minnesota. Connie lives in Oregon. We have never met. Yet, we came together through a mutual connection to write this book—each utilizing and maximizing our unique talents, specific strengths, and areas of expertise. Martha is a Gallup-Certified Strengths Coach through the Gallup organization. Connie is a certified Project Management Professional through the Project Management Institute (PMI®).

Using the CliftonStrengths® talent assessment, our top five talent themes are:

| Connie | Martha |
|---|---|
| Input® | Responsibility® |
| Maximizer® | Connectedness® |
| Achiever® | Learner® |
| Focus® | Belief® |
| Harmony® | Achiever® |

Note that we have one in common—Achiever®. Our Achiever® talents drive us to get things done! We also have different dominant talent themes that we use in our strengths-based complementary partnership! And so this book came to life.

Our thanks. A special thank you to our mutual friend and professional colleague, Tim Kloppenborg, who had the wisdom and foresight to put us together as complementary partners to write this book. His passion for combining project management and strengths development has been our inspiration for *"Developing Strengths-Based Project Teams."* We greatly appreciate and value Tim's endless support, answering countless of questions, and being our champion for this endeavor. Without you, Tim, this book would not have happened!

# CHAPTER 1

# Introduction: The How and the Why

Welcome to **Developing Strengths-Based Project Teams!**

*We do our best work when we love what we do!*

Think about your project team. Each of your team members brings their talents and their project management (PM) tool kit to your project team. Their "kit" contains their own project management knowledge, concepts, skills, experiences, competencies, and expertise. Although each team member's PM tool kit may contain common tools, each team member has a unique combination of tools.

Your team members also have unique talents, which they have developed and have the potential to further develop. Your collective project team's unique talents combined with their collective PM tool kits are what equip your team to be successful—to complete the project on time, within budget, and according to the project objectives and specifications.

The purpose of this book is to help you and your project team members add *talent development tools* to your existing PM tool kits to maximize the use of your team's collective talents and project management tools. As your project team members invest talent development into their PM tool kits and combine talent development with their other project management tools, your project team will be better equipped to maximize and leverage each team member's talents toward your project's objectives, deliverables, tasks, and challenges.

The purpose of this chapter is to help you:

1. Look ahead to the strengths-based talent development content in the book

2. Explore the short-term and long-term benefits of strengths-based project teams

3. Get an overview of foundational strengths development building blocks

4. Understand that the book's content can be adapted to fit your unique project team

## Who Is This Book for?

This book is written for those engaged in project management from a variety of organizations:

- For-profit corporations
- Non-profit service organizations
- Government agencies
- Education institutions

This book is written for project managers, project teams, and those who want to learn about how to engage in and/or support project team strengths-based talent development; therefore, the book's intended audience includes:

- Project managers and project team members
  - Experienced project managers/team members
  - Individuals who are relatively new to project management and have a basic project management knowledge base
- Project sponsors
- Individuals and consultants who facilitate project team development and team meetings
- Educators and students studying project management and team development strategies
- Anyone working in a project team environment (virtual or in-person)

If you are currently in a project management role, you may wear different "hats" on different project teams. On one team, you might be the project manager. On other teams, you might be a team member or a subject matter expert. Or if you are in a leadership or executive role, you might be the project sponsor. Or you may have a completely different project management role. The context of your project team may also vary. You may be working on a co-located team, where everyone is in the same place, or be working on a virtual team, where everyone is remote. Regardless of your organization type, specific project management role, or project team context, you will be able to directly apply this book's "why" and "how" of strengths-based project team development in your project management role.

> This book is intended for long-term **project teams** rather than for *general teams*. A "general" team is a team where all team members directly report to the team's manager as compared to a project team member who may directly report to their functional manager instead of the project manager. The project team works as a team until the completion of their project. (Read more about the definition of project teams and related project team terminology in Chapter 2.)

While the book's content and processes are written for *long-term project teams*, project teams working on *short-term projects* can also benefit from using some of the exercises in the book *if* each project team member has had prior experience with individual strengths-based talent development (Chapters 3 and 4). The greatest benefit for short-term project teams using strengths-based talent development is to help the team members get to know each other *fast*—for building relationships quickly.

Finally, this book assumes its readers have at least a basic understanding of project management; however, readers *do not* need to have a background in strengths-based talent development.

## What Is Strengths-Based Talent Development for Project Teams?

There are different talent development models and approaches available to you and your project team. Because of our experiences and successes using the strengths-based talent development approach with teams, we have chosen to use the strengths-based talent development model in this book for explaining:

- Why talent development is important for project teams
- How to integrate a talent development model into your team members' PM tool kits
- How to practice applying and sustaining the use of talent development practices on the project team

Through the lens of strengths-based talent development, talents are the ways a person naturally "thinks, feels, and behaves"[1]—what a person naturally does best. Strengths-based project teams are highly effective, high-performing teams who invest in their talents to develop their strengths and maximize the strengths that each project team member brings to the team. Strengths-based project managers know, understand, and utilize their own strengths and the strengths of their project team members.

As your project team members integrate a strengths-based talent development approach into their PM tool kits, your project team can become a strengths-based project team and create a strengths-based project team culture. A strengths-based project team culture nurtures an environment in which team members can use their talent development tools for the long-term, developing and applying what they naturally do best, resulting in higher project team performance.

## What Key Talent Development Tools Will You Add to Your PM Tool Kit?

As you read and engage in the exercises in this book, you will learn about foundational talent development principles, building blocks, processes, and practices, which will equip you to begin to engage in individual and project team strengths-based talent development. The key strengths-based talent development understandings, knowledge, and skills that you will gain from this book and be able to add to your PM tool kit include:

- Understanding *why* strengths development and application are important for project teams
- Exploring core strengths development concepts as they relate to project teams

- Integrating project management techniques with strengths-based talent development
- Incorporating individual and project team strengths-based talent development exercises
- Creating and sustaining a strengths-based project team culture
- Locating additional resources and templates for strengths-based talent development

The beginning of each chapter includes the chapter's **purpose**—to provide you with the chapter's focus and direction. At the end of each chapter, there are **key questions**—to help you reflect on and apply the chapter's content to your project team. Many of the chapters also refer you to **resources** to further explore and learn about strengths-based talent development for your project team.

The following descriptions briefly describe each chapter and appendix:

**Chapter 1 is Introduction:** The Why and the How. This chapter introduces strengths-based talent development for project teams, explains the benefits of becoming a high-performance, strengths-based project team, and emphasizes the adaptability of this book's content for project teams (including virtual teams). It sets the stage.

**Chapter 2 is Definitions:** Staying Aligned. This chapter identifies the key project management terms used throughout the book to provide clarity and briefly introduces various PM terms connected to *strengths-based* project team talent development. The chapter also includes ways to align expectations on a strengths-based project team.

**Chapter 3 is History:** An Overview of Strengths Philosophy and Strengths-Based Project Teams. This chapter provides an overview of the history and philosophy behind high-performance strengths-based teams. Chapter 3 also introduces key strengths-based talent development building blocks and elements to give you a solid strengths foundation for engaging in individual strengths-based talent development presented in Chapter 4.

**Chapter 4 is Starting Point:** Developing your Strengths as a Project Manager. This chapter gives you a framework in identifying that strengths-based project teams start with the strengths of the project manager. Since utilizing the strengths of the project manager is the foundation for leading the project team, the chapter guides project managers in the process of first investing-in and developing their own talents and strengths by using the CliftonStrengths® (StrengthsFinder®) talent assessment tool. Once vested in strengths development, a project manager can then be an effective strengths-based leader, role model, and facilitator for their project team.

**Chapter 5 is Mapping:** Connecting Strengths and Project Management. This chapter provides specific project management examples and a connection map for applying the CliftonStrengths' language of talent to project management.

**Chapter 6 is Process:** Cultivating a Strengths-Based Project Team. This chapter equips the project manager to create a strengths-based project team culture in which project team members can engage in their own strengths development, develop an awareness of each other's talents and strengths, and support each other in maximizing the collective strengths of the team. The project manager will also learn ways in which to facilitate the project team's integration of strengths-based team development with project management principles and techniques in order to leverage the collective strengths of the project team toward successfully completing their project. The chapter includes exercises and a "four-step investment" process for applying the project team's collective strengths.

**Chapter 7 is Sustaining:** Keeping a Strengths-Based Project Team Culture Going. This chapter showcases the important roles of the project sponsor, project manager, functional managers, and project team members to *lead by example* for sustaining a strengths-based project team culture.

**Chapter 8 is Action Plan:** Make an Investment. This chapter provides suggested actions in moving forward and the value in utilizing the project team's collective strengths to achieve project success through developing a strengths-based *focused action plan*.

**Appendix A is Resources:** Useful Resources for your Career and Project Team Development. This section identifies additional resources for helping you to know *where to go from here* and how to *learn more* to further invest strengths-based talent development into your project team.

**Appendix B is Templates and Examples:** Samples and Forms. This section provides several sample forms and templates for your reference and use, along with completed examples as a guide.

**Appendix C is Mapping:** Connecting the 34 CliftonStrengths Themes to Project Management. This chart was developed by Timothy Kloppenborg, author of *Contemporary Project Management*, for connecting specific talents to project management. It is a great reference tool.

**Appendix D is Questions:** Strengths Conversational Prompts for Project Teams. This section gives you suggested questions and ideas to help you and your project team members begin engaging in strengths conversations.

Many of the chapters include specific project management talent development exhibits, exercises, templates, and examples, which are a result of our combined experiences of managing projects, working on and with teams, teaching project management, strengths coaching, and working with our colleagues and students.

Exhibit 1.1 gives you an overview of the book's foundation blocks for project team strengths-based talent development. Throughout this book, we will be referencing these foundation blocks:

Keep this chart handy for easy reference!

- Starting with having a solid strengths development **foundation**, then
- Engaging in **individual** strengths development (Blocks 1, 2, and 3), then
- Moving into **project team** strengths development (Blocks 4, 5, and 6)

*What does this book not include?* This book *does not* cover general project management mechanics or fundamentals and *does not* train strength coaches to become certified project managers. This book *does not* contain the full range of talent development resources available to you, it *does not* replace Gallup, Inc. individual and team strengths-based development materials, and it *does not* train project managers to become certified strengths coaches. If you are interested in adding additional strengths-based talent development tools to your tool kit that are beyond the scope of this book, see Appendix A for information about locating Gallup strengths-based talent development resources and training.

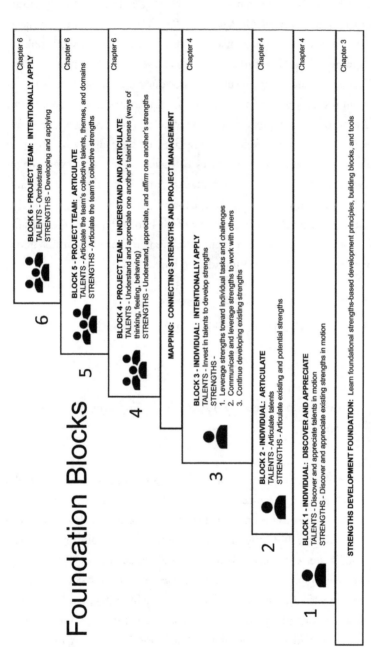

Exhibit 1.1 *Foundation blocks for strengths-based development for project teams*

## Why Strengths-Based Talent Development for Project Teams?

You and each of your project team members have strengths. Maximizing the use of those strengths toward your project will contribute to your project team's success. To explore some specific ways that your project team's use of their strengths could benefit your project team and organization, we need to first define a *strength*.

Think of three things that you do consistently well and list them here:

1. _____

2. _____

3. _____

Congratulations! You have just listed three of your strengths.

A ***strength*** is the ability to "provide consistent, near-perfect performance in a given activity."[2] A strength is talent mixed with several other ingredients, which are shown in the following *Circle of Strength* (Exhibit 1.2). Over your lifetime, you have intentionally invested the circles' other ingredients into your talents to develop the strengths you listed earlier. As you read this book and engage in the book's exercises, you will gain a deeper understanding of talents, strengths, and the "ingredients to develop strengths."

We can now dive into the benefits of strengths-based development for project teams. Benefits gained are identifiable when projects are

STRENGTH

*Exhibit 1.2 Circle of strength*

undertaken and successfully completed to create change or improvements in the organization. When teams invest strengths-based talent development into their team, the benefits they gain are often increased productivity and profitability, a bottom-line impact for for-profit corporations or greater value-add for service companies, non-profit organizations, education institutions, and government agencies. When project team members intentionally integrate their knowledge, skills, and practice of strengths development with project management tools and techniques, the project team is better equipped to apply and maximize their collective strengths for successfully completing their project on time, within budget, and according to the project objectives and specifications.

The formation of project teams can take different avenues. Ideally, the project manager and team members are hand-selected by the project sponsor because of their extensive experience, unique skills, and valuable expertise. However, sometimes team members are "thrown together" because people are available. Or a team member may be selected for a project team because they sit within 20 feet of the project manager's desk!

Most of the time, project teams are temporary: A project team forms, team members work toward and complete their project, and then the project team disperses. At the end of the project, the project team members either go back to their "regular work" or they move on to the next

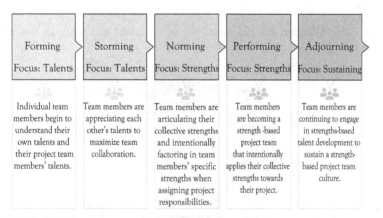

Exhibit 1.3 *Applying strengths-based talent development in the Tuckman team development model*

project, the next phase, or the next team. Even when projects occur over multiple years, project team members come and go.

Regardless of how the project team comes together or how long the project team exists, the team needs to get to the "performing" stage quickly, the fourth stage of Bruce Tuckman's team development model. Tuckman's model "combines both task-related and people-related activities"[3] in five stages: forming, storming, norming, performing, and adjourning. These "stages of team development are seen as a linear progression.... As one moves from the forming stage toward the performing stage, team performance and productivity are likely to improve."[4]

Strengths-based project team development integrates well with Tuckman's model as shown in Exhibit 1.3.

Strengths-based project teams have the potential to quickly become high-performing project teams. When project team members are investing in strengths development and using common talent language to understand and value each other's *talents*, they can get to know each other quickly and work more efficiently together. Therefore, in the forming and storming stages, a strengths-based project team focuses on understanding and appreciating their own and each other's **talents**, in order to maximize the team's ability to collaborate well.

Once project team members have a solid foundation in strengths development and understand and appreciate their project team members' talents, then the project team is ready to articulate and apply their **collective strengths** to their project in the norming and performing stages. The project team uses their combined PM tool kits and *collective strengths* toward their project. The strengths-based project team naturally integrates strengths conversations into their formal and informal meetings toward addressing challenges and more effective planning and decision making.

Finally, in the adjourning stage, the strengths-based project team is developing their ability to **sustain** their strengths-based project team culture and potentially cultivate a strengths-based talent development culture for their future project teams and toward lifelong people development.

Lifelong people development is a natural "good" consequence of project teams investing in strengths-based talent development. Like planting a seed, cultivating the soil, adding water, sun, and attention, the seed will grow—and so will project team members as they continually learn and intentionally apply their talents and strengths. In the process of creating a culture for valuing and using strengths, people will further develop. As people *use* their talents and strengths, they become *more adept* at using their talents and strengths for further strengths-based development and application. And as strengths-based project teams develop and apply their collective talents and strengths, they will be more likely to successfully achieve their team and organization's goals.

Furthermore, project team members could potentially include strengths-based team development in their future project teams and/or support their project sponsor in future projects to form other highly effective strengths-based project teams—creating a ripple effect. Therefore, a strengths-based project team has the potential to influence a *strengths-based* cultural shift within their organization.

Ralph Waldo Emerson, American lecturer and poet, wrote: "The mind, once stretched by a new idea, never returns to its original dimensions."[5] The same is true with developing and applying your talents and strengths. Once you and your project team begin to discover, appreciate, articulate, and intentionally apply your talents and strengths, you will never go back to your "original dimensions." You will continue to grow and further develop as a high-performing, strengths-based project team.

## Adaptability

One of the qualities of an effective project team is being resourceful and adaptable. The benefit in applying your talents and strengths to a project team is that there is no "one set approach." Projects are unique, project teams are unique, and individuals are unique. Each person discovers, understands, appreciates, articulates, and intentionally applies their talents and strengths in different ways.

Think about the project teams you have managed or been a member of—most likely, there were no two projects, no two project teams, and/or no two project team members exactly alike. Therefore, the best talent development action plan for each unique project team will be slightly different. Instead of giving you a "one size fits all" talent development action plan or general "checklist" about how your project team *should* develop and apply their talents and strengths, this book will guide you in the process of adapting this material for your unique project team.

As we guide you along the way, you will be applying your own creativity and resourcefulness to the "how" in applying this material, customizing the book's tools and techniques, and creating an action plan for your unique project team. In addition, engagement in your own talent development will begin to equip you to understand and develop a best *talent development action plan* for your unique project team. And as you use the book's content to develop your current project team, you will also be acquiring transferable, adaptable talent development tools that you can apply to future project teams.

Becoming a strengths-based project team takes time, practice, and intentionality; therefore, as you read this book, keep in mind that:

***This is just the beginning...*** This is the "tip of the iceberg" in gaining knowledge about strengths-based project teams. As a project professional, you are a continuous learner. Just as you continue to grow your project management knowledge and experiences, we encourage you to also continue to grow your strengths-based knowledge and integrate strengths development with project management.

***Take time to process...*** This book is not intended to be read cover-to-cover in one sitting. Take time to do the exercises, write some notes, reflect on your own projects and project teams, and think of ways you can apply the various strengths development tools and techniques to your personal development and professional environments. Do not rush through the book. You will gain more value if you pause to reflect and take time to process the book's content to fit your needs.

***We invite you to open dialogue...*** As you read and apply this information, we welcome your input, questions, and feedback. We would love to hear from you about how you apply the book's information and processes, the results you have from applying this content, and/or any case studies you would like to share with us.

## Summary

You are embarking on a journey of integrating talent development with project management. This book will help you and your project team to learn how to invest a strengths-based talent development model into your PM tool kit. Combining the strengths-based talent development approach with other project management tools will equip you to become a strengths-based project manager and your project team to become a strengths-based project team. While there are short-term and long-term benefits which result from project management strengths-based talent development, the lifetime benefit is people development. The book's strengths-based building blocks and principles will provide you with the foundation for strengths development—for you and your project team. As you read about and engage in the book's concepts and exercises, we encourage you to tailor the book's content to fit your unique project needs and environments. Let the journey begin!

## Key Questions

1. In this chapter, you listed three of your strengths—things that you do consistently well. Can you list more of your strengths?
2. What short-term and long-term benefits do you see in developing and sustaining strengths-based project teams in your organization?
3. Since we each have unique talents and strengths, what specific approaches in applying your talents and strengths will work for you? How would you incorporate these approaches in working with your project team?

## Notes

1. Rath (2007, p. 20).
2. Rath (2007, p. 20).
3. Anantatmula (2016, p. 49).
4. Anantatmula (2016, p. 49).
5. Goodreads (2018).

## References

Anantatmula, V.S. 2016. *Project Teams: A Structured Development Approach.* New York, NY: Business Expert Press.

Goodreads. 2018. https://goodreads.com/quotes/37815-the-mind-once-stretched-by-a-new-idea-never-returns (accessed March 24, 2018).

Harter, J., and M. Buckingham. 2016. *First, Break All The Rules: What the World's Greatest Managers Do Differently.* New York, NY: Gallup Press.

Rath, T. 2007. *StrengthsFinder 2.0.* New York, NY: Gallup Press.

Tuckman, B.W. 1965. "Developmental Sequence in Small Groups." *Psychological Bulletin* 63, pp. 384–99.

# CHAPTER 2

# Definitions: Staying Aligned

Strengths-based project teams integrate their knowledge, skills, and practice of strengths development with project management tools and techniques, equipping the project team to apply and maximize their collective strengths to successfully complete their project on time, within budget, and according to the project objectives and specifications.

This book integrates common project management and strengths-based talent development language to help you and your project team learn about and become a *strengths-based project team*. Project managers and project team members use specific project management terms; however, in some situations (e.g., global project teams), these common terms can have slightly different meanings to different project teams and/or team members. Therefore, to help you prepare to learn about strengths-based project team development, this chapter defines key project management terms that are used in this book and introduces various PM terms connected to strengths-based project teams.

The purpose of this chapter is to help you:

1. Define specific terminology used in this book to provide clarity and alignment
2. Understand the project manager's talent development role as a coach and facilitator
3. Demonstrate how to align expectations on a project team

## Keywords

The key project management terms used in this book are listed as follows. For ease of reference, the key terms are listed in alphabetical order:

- Coaching
- Functional manager
- Mentoring
- Project management
- Project management (PM) tool kit
- Project manager
- Project sponsor
- Project team
- Stakeholder
- Strengths-based project team
- Talent development
- Team development
- Team member

We briefly define the key terms in the following section. In addition to the "standard definitions," for some of the terms we have also included roles and responsibilities that are relevant in developing strengths-based project teams.

To learn more about the terms, please refer to *A Guide to the Project Management Body of Knowledge* (PMBOK® Guide) published by the Project Management Institute and strengths-based talent development resources listed in Appendix A.

## Coaching

Coaching is a form of development in which a person called a *coach* supports a learner or client in achieving a specific personal or professional goal by providing training and guidance. In other words, coaching is helping another individual to develop specific skills to reach their goals. The person doing the coaching is the *coach* and the learner is the *coachee*. Occasionally, *coaching* may mean an informal relationship between two people, of whom one has more experience and expertise than the other and the former offers advice and guidance as the latter learns.

Coaching differs from mentoring: coaching focuses on specific developmental tasks or objectives, whereas mentoring focuses on more general goals for overall development.

In project coaching, the coach guides others in developing skills that will benefit the project and the team.

In strengths-based talent development coaching, the role of the coach is to equip individuals and teams with knowledge of strengths-based talent development principles, exercises, and conversations for developing an awareness of their talents and strengths. The talent development coach then guides the individual or team in the process of naming action items to apply their talents/strengths toward their goals.

## Functional Manager

The functional manager is considered the individual who has management authority over an employee. A functional manager is an employee's boss or supervisor, and the employee is the functional manager's "direct report." Often it is the functional manager who has assigned their direct report to the project team or has given their employee permission to work on the project. It is the functional manager's responsibility to ensure that their direct report has the right skills and training, dedicated time, and adequate resources to be a key contributor on the project team.

The functional manager plays an important role in their direct report's development, including their direct report's strengths-based talent development.

## Mentoring

Mentorship is a learning and development partnership between someone with vast experience and someone who wants to learn. It is a relationship in which a more experienced or more knowledgeable person helps to guide a less experienced or less knowledgeable person. The mentor may be older or younger than the person being mentored, but he or she must have a certain area of expertise.

Strengths-based mentoring includes modeling, creating an environment for strengths-based workplaces, and encouraging strengths-based conversations.

# Project Management

Project management is "the application of knowledge, skills, tools, and techniques to project activities to meet the project requirements."[1] It is the combination and utilization of these elements that help project managers and project team members to effectively and successfully complete the project.

# Project Management (PM) Tool Kit

Project managers and project team members build their project management (PM) tool kits over time. Just like a carpenter, who carries a tool box with a hammer, screwdriver, and other specific carpentry "tools," a project manager and each project team member have acquired common and unique tools that fit in various "compartments" in their PM tool kit.

Each project team member's PM tool kit includes a unique combination of specific project management knowledge, experiences, skills, concepts, approaches, techniques, tools, and resources that the team member has acquired, has learned to use, and continues to add to over time. Project team members do not use all their tools at the same time; instead, they select the tools they need depending on the size and complexity of the project and the project management maturity and experience of the team members.

In addition to using project management tools for managing projects, successful project managers are adept in tailoring and re-purposing their project management tools for other uses.

Throughout this book, we encourage you to create a strengths-based talent development compartment in your PM tool kit, in which you can add key learnings that you have acquired from this book.

# Project Manager

The project manager is the individual responsible for delivering the project objective and leads the team throughout the project.

A strengths-based project manager's role includes creating a project team environment in which project team members can individually and collectively engage in strengths-based talent development. It is important that the project manager first understands his/her own talent themes and strengths before the project manager can help other team members "buy-in" and support the development of their strengths-based project team.

## Project Sponsor

Have you ever worked on a project without a sponsor? Someone, someplace, authorized the project.

The project sponsor can be an individual, a group of people or department, or an organization who has authorized the project team to do the project. The project sponsor has ultimate control over the project, in that it is the project sponsor who provides the resources, funding, permission, and support to do the project. Depending on the size of the project, the sponsor may have had an informal or formal role.

In some organizations, the project sponsor provides the funding for project team development, including talent development. Ideally, the project sponsor plays an important role in ensuring that there is an organizational culture that supports and sustains strengths-based project teams.

## Project Team

The project team consists of individuals or groups who are working together to deliver the project objective and support the project manager. For purposes of this book, we refer to the project team as *all* individuals working together on the project team to achieve project success. This includes the project manager, team members, subject matter experts, project coordinator, technical leads, and others who are members of the project core team.

Most often, project team members come from different departments in the organization and even outside the organization. Therefore, generally project team members do not report directly to the project manager; instead, each project team member has a functional manager.

## Stakeholder

A stakeholder can be a person, a group of people, or an organization who has a vested interest in the project and can be affected—either positively or negatively—by the project decisions and results. Aligning expectations and effectively communicating with stakeholders are key in successful projects.

## Strengths-Based Project Team

A strengths-based team has an awareness and appreciation of each team member's talents and strengths. Team members can then use their individual talents and strengths to intentionally and collaboratively leverage the team's collective strengths to complete team tasks, address team challenges, and achieve the team's performance goals.

Strengths-based project teams integrate their knowledge, skills, and practice of strengths development with project management tools and techniques, equipping the project team to apply and maximize their collective strengths to successfully complete their project on time, within budget, and according to the project objectives and specifications.

## Talent Development

Talent development is developing the *talent potential* in people, so that people can maximize their potential and contribute their developed talents toward their organization's mission, objectives, goals, and tasks. Organizations that offer talent development believe that each member has valuable talents to contribute to their organization, and each member needs to be equipped to know "how" to invest in their talents and given the opportunity to do what they do best every day. Talent development is a key ingredient for strong organizational engagement.

There are various approaches and tools to use for individual and team talent development. This book will focus on strengths-based talent development, which is founded on positive psychology.

## Team Development

Team development equips a team to collaborate well (internally and externally) and maximize its productivity. There are various team development approaches and processes. For example, a common model for team development is the Tuckman model of forming, storming, norming, performing, and adjourning.[2] (See Chapter 1 for applying strengths-based team development in the Tuckman model.)

This book applies the strengths-based team talent development model to project teams, which includes equipping team members to value and develop their own talents and strengths, appreciate their colleagues' talents and strengths, and then apply their project team's collective strengths to their project.

## Team Member

Each team member brings value to the team and works collaboratively with the other team members toward the team's goals.

As a member of a strengths-based team, a team member must first discover, appreciate, articulate, and intentionally apply their individual talents and strengths. Then the team member can apply their strengths collaboratively with the other team members toward the team's goals.

## The Project Manager: Talent Development Coach and Facilitator

There is some overlap between the role of a coach and a facilitator. A coach is someone who walks with a person or group as they engage in personal and/or team development. A talent development coach guides individuals in the process of articulating, developing, and using their talents. A talent development coach also coaches teams to engage in talent development for maximizing the team's ability to apply their collective talents toward the team's goals.

A facilitator is someone who guides a group through a discussion. Often, facilitators use curriculum that helps them to guide their group's discussion. In talent development, a facilitator creates an "environment" for group members to engage talent development discussions to *help each other* in the process of articulating, developing, and using their talents. Therefore, the facilitator helps the group members to become informal "coaches" for one another. Being a facilitator is one component of a talent development coach's role.

Can a project manager be a talent development facilitator and coach for their project team? Yes! A standard role of a project manager is to "facilitate" a project team meeting to ensure the team meetings are focused and effective, keeping the project (and team) moving forward. When project teams engage in talent development, the project manager has a key role to create the environment for talent development discussions in order for team members to help one another in the process of talent development and maximize the team's collective talents.

Project managers may also serve in some capacity as a talent development coach for their project team, providing opportunities for individual and team talent development learning and exercises. Unless a project manager attends a formal talent development training course, they will need some managerial talent development coaching and/or curriculum to use as they coach their project team and facilitate team talent development discussions.

The purpose of this book is to give you an introduction to one form of a talent development process—strengths-based talent development. The book will equip you to facilitate and guide your project team as the team begins investing in strengths-based talent development. After you and your team begin your initial investment, you may decide to seek formal strengths-based talent development training for yourself or hire a trained strengths-based talent development coach to help your team to dive deeper into talent development. Appendix A includes information about how to acquire more strengths-based talent development curriculum, coaching, and training.

## Aligning Expectations

For project teams to maximize the use of their combined talents, strengths, and PM tool kits toward their project, project teams need to align expectations. How often do you hear from project team members, "Well, I didn't know that was expected of me!?" The process of identifying "shared expectations" is an activity that project teams can use to *share* their expectations and commitments to one another on the project team, including their commitment to developing and using their talents and strengths on the team.

As your project team members enter into a new working relationship as a project team, use the shared expectations exercise for getting started as a project team. Ideally, the shared expectations exercise is best used at a project kick-off meeting or early in the project. Everyone on the project team is a key contributor and needs to be an active participant in the exercise.

The shared expectations exercise is done as a project team where the team members are asking questions, clarifying the responses, and documenting the results. Consider using a flipchart or white board. If you are a virtual team, use a virtual white board or interactive tool to capture the discussion. Exhibit 2.1 can be used as a sample.

Step 1: Start with the project manager. State clearly: "As your Project Manager, here is what you can expect from me. I will start meetings on time; I will end on time. There will be an agenda distributed 48 hours in advance...."

- Continue to add your unique inputs.
- Wrap-up Step 1 by asking: "What else are you expecting from me, as your project manager?"

*Exhibit 2.1* **Shared expectations document**

| What are your expectations of me as the project manager? | What are my expectations of you as a team member? | As a team member of this group, what are your expectations of each other? |
|---|---|---|
| • I will start meetings on time<br>• I will end meetings on time<br>• I will distribute the agenda 48 hours in advance of meeting<br>• I will provide opportunities for our project team to become aware of our collective strengths<br>• I will encourage all team members to develop and use their strengths on the team | • I will complete my tasks on time<br>• I will reach out if I have questions<br>• I will utilize my talents and strengths toward the project<br>• I will articulate my talents, PM tool kit, and strengths that I bring to the team<br>• I will learn about and value the strengths of my fellow team members<br>• I will continue to develop my project management strengths | • We will reach out for help if needed<br>• We will resolve problems among ourselves<br>• We will support one another<br>• We will learn from each other<br>• We will engage in strengths conversations to further develop our strengths as a team<br>• We will value what each team member brings to the team<br>• We will apply our collective strengths as a team |

Step 2: Turn to each team member and ask: "As a member of this team, what can I expect from you?"

The team member may reply with items like: "I will complete my assigned tasks on time. I will reach out if I have questions. I will utilize my talent themes and strengths...."

- Continue to capture inputs from each team member.
- Wrap-up Step 2 by asking: "Is there anything else that you would like to add?"

Step 3: Turn to the group and collectively ask: "As a team member of this group, what are your expectations of each other?"

The group may reply with items like: "We will reach out for help when needed. We will resolve problems among ourselves. We will support one another. We will learn from each other. We will encourage each other to use our strengths...."

- Continue to capture inputs from the group.
- End the discussion by asking: "Is there anything else to consider?"

The results of your discussion may look like what is shown in Exhibit 2.1.

Once all commitments are captured on a flipchart or virtual white board, transfer the commitments to a written document. This is called a *shared expectations* document. The shared expectations document should be one page.

After creating the shared expectations document, every project team member needs to sign (or concur with) the document, which will confirm that everyone is "buying in" to the commitments listed.

At the end of the exercise, the team agrees and understands their commitments. Everyone knows what is expected of them and what they can expect from the project team and the other team members.

The shared expectations document is posted where readily available for reference by the project team or individuals involved. The document is added to your other project team documents, such your project plan and ground rules for meetings.

The shared expectations document is similar yet different from a team charter. A team charter is focused on many aspects of the project. While a team charter may describe how you are going to work together as a project team, it could also include items like the team's mission, project objective, roles, responsibilities, decision making process, and many other elements. A team charter provides a much larger "picture" for the project team. Whereas, the shared expectations exercise is focused on one thing—expectations! What are the mutual expectations of being part of this team? It is a great exercise to jumpstart your work together! It is a tool that has worked well for many project managers on many projects— regardless of the size or complexity of the project.

In Appendix B, you will find a template and completed example for your use. Like many project management tools, the tools are adaptable to be used in any team environment. You can use this exercise in a mentor/ mentee relationship, as a functional manager with your direct report, as a President working with a Board of Directors, and with other types of teams. The shared expectations tool is intended to be modified to fit your team's needs.

## Summary

Having alignment on key terms is critical for effective communication and understanding. This chapter gives you a high-level overview of key words and terms, which we will be referring to throughout the book. As you continue reading this book, we encourage you to refer back to this chapter for clarity. Check out the Project Management Institute resources and other resources listed in Appendix A for additional information about key project management and strengths-based talent development terminology.

This book will help a project manager begin the process of facilitating talent development for their team. Other strengths-based talent development resources and training are also available to the project manager and located in Appendix A.

Aligning expectations at the start of the project to ensure that expectations stay aligned throughout the life of the project will also help you maximize the strengths of your project team. Use the "shared expectations" exercise to help you align your project team's expectations.

After you conducted the shared expectations exercise, you may never hear again "Well, I didn't know that was expected of me!"

## Key Questions

1. If you have worked on global project teams, where team members use multiple languages, live in different time zones, and/or are located around the world, think of project management terms that your teams have used that have been challenging for team members to gain alignment. What can you do in the future to improve communication or terminology understanding?
2. Describe your experiences of facilitating or coaching project teams. What situations were challenging? What situations were successful? Describe the challenging and successful situations. As you reflect on your experiences, what can you do to improve facilitating and coaching your current and future project teams?
3. What methods or approaches have you used to align expectations among teams, stakeholders, or even with your functional manager? What worked well? What could have been improved?

## Notes

1. PMBOK® Guide (2017, p. 716).
2. Tuckman (1965, pp. 384–99).

## References

PMBOK® Guide. 2017. *A Guide to the Project Management Body of Knowledge*, 6th ed. Newtown Square, PA: Project Management Institute.

Tuckman, B.W. June 1965. "Developmental Sequence in Small Groups." *Psychological Bulletin* 63, pp. 84–99.

# CHAPTER 3

# History: An Overview of Strengths Philosophy and Strengths-Based Project Teams

This chapter is an overview of key principles and processes in strengths-based talent development that we believe are essential tools for developing strengths-based project teams.

The purpose of this chapter is to help you:

1. Begin adding strengths development tools to your project management (PM) tool kit.
2. Understand foundational strengths development building blocks for individual strengths-based development.
3. Understand the characteristics of a strengths-based project team.
4. Have the general framework of this book's strengths-based process for developing a strengths-based project team.

Besides this book, are there more strengths-based talent development resources available to you? Yes! Chapter 3 is simply an overview; therefore, we highly recommend that you read additional strengths-based books and online articles for more extensive explanation, examples, and exercises, which will help you to engage in a deeper understanding of strengths-based development principles and building blocks. (See Appendix A for a list of other resources).

# Foundational Individual Strengths Development Building Blocks

The strengths-development building blocks for *individual strengths-based development* summarized in this section will give you a general foundation required to understand and engage in *strengths-based project team* development.

### History of Strengths-Based Development

Dr. Donald Clifton was a positive psychologist and is often referred to as the Father of Strengths Psychology. Instead of focusing on what is "wrong" with people, Dr. Clifton was interested in what is "right" with people. In his research, he interviewed many people, asking them questions about what they liked doing, when they are happiest, and when they are most successful. He discovered that people are happiest and most successful when they can use their **strengths** every day. Through his research he learned that the foundation for a person's strengths are their **talents**—the ways a person naturally thinks, feels, and behaves.[1]

After extensive interviewing and reviewing of data, Dr. Clifton and his colleagues named **34 CliftonStrengths® Themes**—*talent themes,* which are groupings or categories of talents. Dr. Clifton and his colleagues then developed the CliftonStrengths (StrengthsFinder®) assessment, the results of which give each person who takes the assessment their **CliftonStrengths Signature Themes**—their *top five dominant talent themes.* Starting in 2001, the CliftonStrengths assessment was made available to the public. As of 2018, over 19 million people around the world have taken the assessment.[2]

Your CliftonStrengths assessment results are a foundational and essential *tool* for you to add to your PM tool kit. As with any tool, it important to read the instruction manual before using the tool. Therefore, this book is somewhat of an abbreviated instruction manual, helping you to understand the purpose of CliftonStrengths assessment results, what the results do and do not do, and ways you could use the results in project management. Chapter 4 will walk you through the process of how to take the assessment and begin using the assessment results.

### The Purpose of the CliftonStrengths (StrengthsFinder) Assessment

The purpose of the CliftonStrengths assessment results is to give people a starting point in which to name their unique and specific dominant talents so that they can be more intentional about describing and articulating their **existing strengths** and developing **new strengths**.

---

The CliftonStrengths assessment results *are not* designed for putting people in "boxes" or "labeling" people—each person's specific talents and strengths are unique!

The assessment results *do not* give people their specific and unique strengths—each person is responsible for naming their many strengths.

The CliftonStrengths results *do* give people a ***basic language*** in which to understand and articulate each of their unique and specific dominant talents, the foundation and key ingredient for each of their many specific strengths.

A general process for articulating your unique and specific dominant talents through the lens of project management will be presented in Chapter 4.

---

## Articulating Talent (Potential)

If talent themes help a person articulate their dominant talents, what exactly is a talent?

Talent is like "potential energy" and is foundational for developing a strength. Strengths-based positive psychology defines dominant talents as "naturally recurring patterns of thought, feeling, or behavior that *can* be productively applied."[3] Although talents have the potential to become strengths, each person, team member, or organizational member needs to intentionally name, invest in, and apply their individual and collective talents to maximize their talent potential.

You can't acquire your talents—you are born with your talents.

"[T]alents naturally exist within you and cannot be acquired. They are your inborn predispositions. They are the things that you do instinctively and that naturally give you satisfaction. Your spontaneous, top-of-mind reactions to the situations you encounter are the best indicators of your talents."[4]

Your talents are like filters helping you to navigate living in the world. Your talents are the ways that you naturally think, feel, and behave. Since you are born with talents, your talents give you lifelong energy and potential: "Human talent may be one of the most sustainable, renewable forms of natural energy."[5]

Here are some examples of specific talents:

- Sees the uniqueness of each team member
- Driven to solve problems
- Sees the positive light in situations or challenges
- Takes the complex and makes it simple
- Enjoys meeting new stakeholders
- Knows how each team member feels
- Drawn toward the process of learning
- Driven to get things checked off the list
- Sees the potential in others
- Takes charge
- Gets things moving
- Gathers lots of information

Your talents influence, affect, "enhance, modify, regulate,"[6] and complement each other. Therefore, when you engage in the process of articulating your specific talents, it is helpful to consider *how* your talents are influencing each other, giving you more insights and ideas about how you can best use and maximize your specific talents' potential. For example, a team member with a dominant talent of "driven to solve problems" may also have a dominant talent for "knowing how each team member feels." This person's talent for "knowing how people feel" may influence her "driven to solve problems" talent, resulting in specific strengths for solving people-related problems.

How can you articulate your specific and unique talents? Your top five CliftonStrengths Themes can begin to help you identify your specific and unique dominant talents. Each of the 34 CliftonStrengths Themes has a general summary describing the theme, which can be found in several Gallup resources, such as *StrengthsFinder 2.0* (see Appendix A). Embedded in each respective theme summary are words and phrases that describe specific talents associated with that theme.

Your top five talent theme summaries can also help you to reflect on and discover ways your dominant talents influence each other, equipping you to be even more specific when articulating your specific talents and strengths.

In Chapter 4, you will be given tools to help you in the process of articulating your specific talents.

## Connecting Talent Themes and Project Management

Often, we are asked, "It's great that I know my top five talent themes, but how do I connect them with project management?" In addition, we frequently work with professionals who are in job transition and are seeking ways to connect their talent themes to project management for showcasing their expertise and strengths on their resume.

At first, it can be a bit overwhelming. There are 34 talent themes. Applying each of themes to project management can lead you in so many different directions. To help make the connection between the talent themes and project management, take a look at Chapter 5 where Timothy Kloppenborg, author of *Contemporary Project Management,* has made an alignment for us. It is a great resource to put in your strengths development compartment of your PM tool kit.

## Developing Strength (Ability and Performance)

If a talent is the foundation for a strength, what exactly is a strength? Although a talent may give a person a general ability or potential to do something, a *talent that has been invested-in* gives a person a specific *strength*—"the ability to consistently provide near-perfect performance" in a given activity.[7] Two key words in this formal definition for strength is ability and performance: having the ability to do something really well and do it consistently well.

Consider these differences between a talent and a strength.  For example:

| Talent—An individual naturally… | Strength—An individual has proficient, consistent ability for… |
| --- | --- |
| Looks for solutions | Solving complex problems |
| Is comfortable with moving parts | Coordinating events |
| Thinks outside the box | Creating new products |
| Sees potential in others | Mentoring others |
| Is objective in approach | Interpreting data for other's understanding |

How can you develop your strengths? People are not born with strengths but develop their strengths over their lifetime. Once a person develops a specific strength, they can then use or leverage that strength toward their tasks, challenges, and goals. In Chapter 4, we will suggest ways for you to name your current strengths and engage in the process of developing further strengths. However, for you to fully name and develop your strengths, you need to know some key elements for developing a strength.

### Key Elements for Developing a Strength

As shown in Exhibit 3.1, consider this equation: **Talent + Knowledge + Skills = Strength**[8]

In addition to the dominant talents anchored in your top five talent themes, knowledge and skills are key ingredients for developing a strength. Although talent *cannot* be acquired, knowledge and skills *can* be acquired.

Where does strengths building begin? It starts with your dominant talents, followed by acquiring specific knowledge and skills and investing the knowledge and skills into your dominant talents.

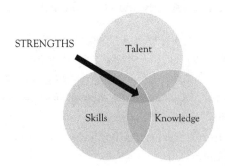

*Exhibit 3.1  Strengths equation*

For the purpose of building strengths, let us define what skills and knowledge mean.

**Skills** are the *step-by-step processes* "to do something" that you have acquired or can acquire from a classroom, a teacher/mentor, a book, and/or online. General skills include touch typing or using software program like Microsoft® Word, Excel, or Project.

**Knowledge** is factual, conceptual, and experiential.

- *Conceptual and factual knowledge*: This is knowledge that you have or can acquire from a classroom setting, a teacher/mentor, a book, and/or online.
- *Experiential knowledge*: This is knowledge you gain from the practice of using what you know. Even your basic day-to-day living gives you experiential knowledge. You acquire experiential knowledge throughout your lifetime as you practice using your talents and acquired knowledge and skills.

As we go forward, we will be using the term "knowledge" to describe conceptual and factual knowledge and the term "experiences" to describe experiential knowledge.

How does this all tie together? Take a look at Exhibit 3.2. You can see how your talents, knowledge, skills, and experiences are all "key elements" in developing your strengths.

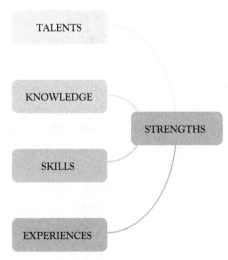

*Exhibit 3.2  Key elements for strengths development*

Over your lifetime, you have already developed some strengths without even intentionally thinking about strengths development. However, to maximize the potential of all your dominant talents, you need to be intentional about the talent investment process. To illustrate the talent investment process, consider the **process of making a loaf of bread**:

What is the foundational ingredient for a loaf of bread? *Flour*

What else is required for the bread dough? *Ingredients such as yeast, sugar, and milk*

What needs to happen once the dough mixture is made? *Kneading and baking*

What is the final product? *A loaf of bread*

Now compare making a loaf of bread to **developing a strength**:

What is the foundational ingredient for a strength? *Talent (flour)*

What else is required to develop a strength? *Knowledge and skills (yeast, sugar, and milk)*

What needs to happen once the strength is developed? *More investment and practice (kneading and baking)*

What is the final product? *A strength (bread)*

As you look ahead to Chapter 6, which focuses on project teams, be thinking about other examples that you can use to help your project team gain greater understanding of strengths development building blocks.

## Project Management Key Elements for Developing Strengths

As we apply the basic strengths equation (Talent + Knowledge + Skills = Strengths) to strengths-based project teams, we can populate the equation with project management specific knowledge, skills, and experience toward developing *specific project management strengths*.

As mentioned in Chapter 2, we define the project team to include the project manager and team members. Project team members are continually adding *specific project management knowledge* and *skills* to their PM tool kits. They then use their acquired tools to gain *specific project management experiences*. The process of acquiring and applying specific project management tools and techniques are maximized when the project team also intentionally invests their project management knowledge, skills, and experiences into their talents for developing specific project management strengths.

In Exhibit 3.3, we take a closer look at the difference between identifying and applying knowledge and skills—through training versus experience.

*Exhibit 3.3 PM conceptual knowledge and skills vs. PM experiential knowledge*

|  | **PM conceptual knowledge and skills** | **PM experiential knowledge** |
|---|---|---|
| Identify | Already have and/or need to acquire | Already have and/or need to acquire |
| Apply/Practice | In the classroom | On the job |
| Example | Attending a PM workshop | Managing a project or participating on a project team |

The benefits of strengths-based project teams acquiring project management tools and techniques include equipping the team to better encourage and mentor their colleagues in both project management development and strengths development.

Acquiring project management tools and techniques also give project team members a solid foundation for participating in further project management training and education to continue to grow (acquire) project management specific knowledge and skills—also a benefit for further strengths development.

Like many professions, the project management profession—managing projects and teams—never stands still and is constantly evolving. There is always something new to learn: different project management approaches, new concepts, unique techniques, tools, and skills. Strengths-based project team members continually acquire project management tools and techniques to further develop their strengths for continuous improvement.

Continuous improvement can come in baby steps—it does not have to happen overnight. As project managers and team members use their project management tools and techniques in small ways and invest them into their talents, these mini-applications will eventually lead to larger applications. These mini-applications have a snowball effect—meaning the growth and results continue to increase over time.

In Chapter 4, we will give you tools for intentionally articulating your specific talents, knowledge, and skills, which will help you in the process of naming your current strengths and developing further strengths. In addition to adding your specific talents and strengths to your PM tool kit, we also encourage you to add your **specific project management knowledge, skills, and experiences** *lists* to your tool kit. Your knowledge and skills lists will be elements for you to use in your own strength development process, improving your ability to communicate with your project team about the specific knowledge and skills that you bring to your team. (Check out the template for your lists in Chapter 4 and Appendix B.)

## Return on Investment

### *Talent×Investment=Strength[9]*

Strengths development focuses on investing in **dominant talents** rather than lesser talents, because there is a **high return on investment** for developing a strength from a dominant talent.

> What exactly is an investment? Investment in strengths development is the time and resources that you dedicate (invest) to continuously build upon your dominant talents, resulting in developing a greater strength.

Let's think more about the strengths development's return on investment through metaphorical examples using picture images and mathematical equations. For mathematically illustrating return on investment in talent (see Exhibit 3.4), we will give talent a numeric range of 1 to 10:1 for lesser talent and 10 for dominant talent. For the following series of

*Exhibit 3.4 Talent return on investment*

|  | Talent | X (times) | Investment | = | Return (score) |
|---|---|---|---|---|---|
| Example 1 | 1 | X | 10 | = | 10 |
| Example 2 | 1 | X | 5 | = | 5 |
| Example 3 | 10 | X | 1 | = | 10 |
| Example 4 | 10 | X | 5 | = | 50 |

examples, we will give investment a value of 1 for no investment and 10 for heavy investment.

**Example 1:** $1 \times 10 = 10 \rightarrow$ Gives us a **Low Return on High Investment.** In this first example, we are investing in a *lesser talent* (1) large amounts of time and resources—a *high investment* (10), which gives us a low return (a score of 10).

It is like building a road through a rocky mountain. The road builders invest a lot of dynamite, heavy machinery and time to make the road flat. The result is a road that some vehicles could use; however, the completed road is unstable and narrow. The resulting road is a low return on the high investment.

*This photo* by unknown author is licensed under *CC BY-SA.*
**Example 1: Before**

*Example 1: After*

**Example 2:** 1×5=5 → Gives us a **Low Return on Investment.**
Now let's change the equation so that we are using a moderate amount
of investment (5). We are investing in a *lesser talent* (1) with *moderate
investment* (5), which gives us an even lower rate on return (a score of 5).

Let's think about our road building project again. Instead of going
*through* the mountain (as in Example 1), we are building a road *over* the
rocky mountain. The road builders may not have dynamite but still use
heavy machinery to try to make the rock flatter. The moderate investment
in building the road does not deliver much of a road. Only a few types
of vehicles could handle driving over this road; therefore, the road is not
consistently useable.

*Example 2: Before*

*This photo* by unknown author is licensed under *CC BY-NC-ND*.
*Example 2: After*

### Example 3: 10×1=10 → No Investment

In this example, we are investing in a *dominant talent* (10) with *low investment* (1), which gives us no return (a score of 10)—the result is unchanged.

*Not investing* in a *dominant talent* is like not investing into the untapped potential of the path: the path remains the path. However, the path is still there and so its potential remains. The path could become a road with moderate investment.

*This photo* by unknown author is licensed under *CC BY-SA*.
*Example 3: Before*

*Example 3: After*

**Example 4:** 10×5=50 → **High Return on Investment.**

This is the ideal example. We want to be achieving the highest rate of return on our investment. How do we do this? We invest in a *dominant talent* (10) with *moderate investment* (5) to give us a high return (a score of 50).

Consider our road project: it is like building a road from a path on flat, solid ground—a strong potential for a road. The road builders do not have to dynamite the path. Their use of heavy machinery to smooth out the path has more of an effect to prepare the land for the road. The builders moderately invest by clearing the trees, laying the asphalt, and providing lights. This road is safe and sustainable and can be used by all vehicles.

*Example 4: Before*

*This photo* by unknown author is licensed under *CC BY-SA.*
*Example 4: After*

---

*Key Learning: When you develop your strengths, hone in on and invest in your dominant talents for maximized return on investment!*

---

## Intentionally Applying Strengths

Understanding strengths development and having an awareness and appreciation of your own and others' talents and strengths are essential components of strengths development; however, strengths development does not stop there. Ultimately, strengths development is about equipping you to intentionally *use* your articulated and developed strengths toward your personal, team, and organizational goals, challenges, and tasks. Subsequent chapters will expand on "how" to apply strengths as a project manager, as a project team member, and collectively as a project team.

## Managing Lesser Talents

Sometimes you might be given tasks that seem to require talents that may not be dominant for you. What is the solution? You can *manage* your lesser talents by:

1. Creatively leveraging your strengths
2. Using support systems
3. Forming complementary partnerships[10]

Creatively **leveraging strengths** in situations where it appears that lesser talents are needed takes practice and reflection. For example, let us consider a project team member who needs to "influence" her team to get things done on time, but she doesn't seem to have any dominant influencing talents to help her to influence others. However, one of her dominant, specific **talents** is her *"drive to get things done efficiently."* Rooted in her talent ("drive to get things done efficiently"), she has developed a **strength**—consistently proficient in *"systematically keeping track of what needs to get done and checking it off her list."* She could leverage her strength (*"systematically keeping track of what needs to get done and checking it off her list"*) to create action items assigned in project team meetings, post the action items in a place that is accessible to all project team members, communicate where the action items are posted, and then create a system for marking each action item complete. Therefore, her strength founded on her "drive to get things done efficiently" talent can also be leveraged to *influence* her team members to get things done on time.

Using **support systems** can also help you in situations where you lack specific talents and strengths. Examples of support systems include using a microphone when you need a booming voice to talk to a large group of people, learning a software program to help you keep track of assignments if you lack talents for retaining details in your head, or keeping a word bank if it is challenging for you to think of the right words when writing a status report or important message to a key stakeholder.

Finally, forming **complementary partnerships** relieves the pressure of having to be good at everything. People are not well-rounded in everything. We have gaps. No project team member has all the talents; therefore, by working with multiple complementary strengths partners, you are better equipped to be successful as you work on a project team. We will expand upon complementary partnerships in the next section, "Key Elements for Strengths-Based Project Teams."

## Key Elements for Strengths-Based Project Teams

Once project team members have a solid knowledge of and engagement in individual strengths-based development, they are equipped to engage with their team in *strengths-based project team development.* Let's look at some key foundational strengths-based team development concepts, which are instrumental for understanding and engaging in the process of creating and sustaining strengths-based project teams (Chapters 6 and 7).

### Themes and Domains: Tools for Strengths-Based Project Teams

Earlier, we explained that the purpose of the CliftonStrengths assessment is to give individuals their dominant talent themes, which gives them a starting point and a basic language in which to articulate and understand their dominant talents. CliftonStrengths Themes are also helpful for teams, because the themes give teams a *common talent language* to use, equipping project team members to develop an awareness and appreciation of each other. The common talent language also enables team members to communicate their strengths and ways they can best contribute to their project team.

For example, short-term project teams and/or project teams with members moving on-and-off the team can use the common talent language tool as they onboard new team members, helping the project team quickly develop an appreciation of each other toward better collaboration. Even project teams that stay together for a long period of time also benefit, because the tool gives the team a common language to explore the collective talents and strengths of the team so that they can best leverage the team's collective strengths as they engage in the process of successfully completing their project.

The benefit of the common talent theme language is helpful for project teams of all sizes. And the larger the team, the more talent themes are represented on the team and can be applied toward the project. However, the benefit of more themes on a team also comes with the challenge of managing more talent themes. Think about the project management formula of communication channels, where $N$ is the number of people on the team.

$$N \times (N-1)/2^{[11]}$$

For example, let's say you have a project team of 8 people. $N$=8. Calculating the previous formula, it would be 8 × (8 − 1)/2 which calculates into 28 communication channels in working with just 8 people!

The same is true when working with our talent themes on a team. The size of the project team affects the potential number of possible talent themes which could be represented by the collective project team members.

Let's take a closer look at this concept. Understanding that each member of the team knows their top 5 dominant talent themes:

- If you are working in a partnership with a team of 2 people, you could be working with up to 10 talent themes, which is not too complicated.
- If you are working on a team of 3 people, you could be working with up to 15 themes, which can be somewhat complicated.
- However, think about a project team of 12 people. You could have all of the 34 themes represented on that team. When a large project team enters into applying the collective strengths of their team, the process could be overwhelming.

What do we do when there are so many talent themes to keep track of on a project team? There is even a simpler language for understanding talent: four CliftonStrengths Domains.[12] Each of the 34 CliftonStrengths Themes belong to one of the four domains: executing, influencing, relationship building, and strategic thinking.

Those with talents in the:

"**Executing** domain know how to make things happen … [and] work tirelessly to get it done. …

**Influencing** [domain] help their team reach a much broader audience … [and] are always selling the team's ideas inside and outside the organization. …

**Relationship Building** [domain] are the essential glue that holds a team together … [and] have the unique ability to create groups and organizations that are much greater than the sum of their parts. …

**Strategic Thinking** [domain] are the ones who keep us all focused on what *could be*. They are constantly absorbing and analyzing information and helping the team make better decisions."[13]

Look in Appendix A for resources about learning how to use the CliftonStrengths Domains with your team.

The four CliftonStrengths Domains can help you to simplify your strengths-based project team conversations for applying the collective strengths of your project team. However, consider these words of caution:

1. **Sometimes teams dive too quickly into talking about the four domains.** Before your project team applies the four-domain template to your team, give your team time for understanding, appreciating, and articulating the talents and strengths of the individual team members. Once each team member has an understanding of their own and their project team members' CliftonStrengths Themes, talents, and strengths, then consider the domains for *applying the collective strengths* of the team.

2. **Just as talent themes are not meant to put people in boxes, the four domains are not meant to put people's dominant talent themes in boxes.** Do you remember the example we used about the project team member who used her strengths anchored in her dominant "driven to get things done" talents to influence her colleagues? Understanding that her dominant talents fall into the executing domain instead of the influencing domain can help the team understand the primary power of her dominant talents; however, her "driven to get things done" talents can still be used to influence others. Therefore, the domains give us a general understanding of the primary power of their respective talent themes, but the domains are also somewhat "permeable" so that their respective themes can be applied in ways that are reflective of the other domains.

### Building Blocks for Developing Strengths-Based Project Teams

Strengths-based project team development builds upon individual strengths development building blocks (i.e., discovering, appreciating, and articulating, plus applying talents, knowledge, skills, experience, and strengths). Once engaged in individual strengths development, project team members have the foundation in which to then understand, appreciate, articulate, and apply their *collective strengths* as a project team and become a *strengths-based project team.*

> A strengths-based project team integrates their knowledge, skills, and practice of strengths development with project management tools and techniques, equipping the project team to apply and maximize their collective strengths to successfully complete their project on time, within budget, and according to the project objectives and specifications.

Project team members' strengths include vast, specific, and collective talent, knowledge, and skills ***that can be productively applied toward the project team's goals.*** In addition to having an awareness of the collective strengths of the team, the team will also gain from having a deeper understanding of each project team member's specific knowledge, skills, and experience to further maximize and leverage the team's collective strengths.

When project team members engage in project team strengths-based building blocks, the project team develops characteristics of a strengths-based project team, which include:

- Share a common mission of moving toward the end goal of completing their project
- Know their own unique and specific talents and strengths
- Invest project management concepts and techniques into their talents for developing project management strengths
- Understand that, as an individual, they each bring something to the team—they are great at some things and not very good at other things
- Use their strengths in their role as an individual contributor and as a member of the project team
- Value and encourage other team members
- Have an awareness and an appreciation of their team member's top five talent themes, dominant talent "filters," and specific strengths

- Believe that they need each other to get the project done
- Work effectively together to apply the collective strengths of their team
- Form strengths-based complementary partnerships
- Know how to and intentionally maximize the team's strengths by orchestrating and leveraging the collective strengths of the team toward the team's project goals

### Complementary Strengths-Based Project Team Partnerships

Complementary strengths-based partnerships are the most fundamental relationships of a strengths-based team, causing team members to have thriving, interdependent relationships for maximizing the collective strengths of the team. Since the "key to strengths-based teams [is] forming complementary partnerships,"[14] project managers and project team members need to understand the principles and elements of strengths-based complementary partnerships.

> "Strengths-based partnerships create a magical outcome—a unique capability that could not be achieved by either person alone. It is the ultimate description of one plus one equals three. It is the teaming of strengths."[15]

Strengths-based complementary partners understand that

"[t]he key to achieving success is not trying to be someone else or striving to be as good as your collaborator at whatever he does best or seeking to be universally proficient. It's in discovering your own exceptional abilities, recognizing your weaknesses, and understanding how someone else's abilities complement your own."[16]

Therefore, strengths-based complementary partners mutually recognize that they have an interdependent relationship with each other and believe that:

- We complement one another's strengths.
- We need each other to get the job done.
- My partner does some things much better than I do, and I do some things much better than my partner does.[17]

Give this real-world example some thought: Partner A is a Gallup-Certified Strengths Coach, who has experience coaching teams. Partner B is a certified Project Management Professional, who has worked on many project teams and teaches project management courses. When Partner A and B work together, they leverage their combined talents, expertise, knowledge, skills, experiences, and strengths toward their project. They believe they need each other to get the job done and know that each partner does some things better than the other. Who are Partners A and B? They are the authors of this book!

Partners A and B work so well together because they enhance the talents and strengths of each other, fill-in the talents and strengths gaps of each other, and collaborate in step-by-step project processes (one person does the first step and another person picks up after the first step is finished).

> Based on the various team environments that you have participated in during your career, can you think of an example where you experienced a "complementary partnership?"

Let us now take a closer look at complementary partnerships within project teams through the following examples.

**Example 1**

A team member is assigned to deliver on a task. He may have the strengths to complete the task. However, by partnering with another team member, the partners may add their combined strengths to the task and speed up its completion with greater quality.

**Example 2**

In the project schedule, there is a dependency where a task cannot start before another task is completed. Team member A is assigned to task 1. Team member B is assigned to task 2. Task 2 is dependent on task 1 being completed. Each of the two team members could be considered comple-mentary partners in that they work together to "hand off" the tasks, to ensure that everything is complete—rather than "throwing it over the wall" for team member B to catch!

**Example 3**

In a RACI chart (responsible, accountable, consulted, and informed), each task has one person "accountable" for the tasks, and other team members who are "responsible" for doing the work. Those who are "responsible" may bring a strength to the task that the "accountable" person does not have. In this example, the complementary partner brings a missing talent/strength to the task.

A word of caution: don't confuse talent/strengths with expertise. Remember that our strengths are our "invested-in talents"—those abili-ties that we have developed from our dominant talents to do things really well. On the other hand, expertise is specific knowledge or skills that we have studied and/or gained in a particular area or field—such as techni-cal expertise. Although expertise and strengths are not the same, we *can* invest our expertise into our talents to develop our strengths.

### *Directing the Project Team's Collective Strengths Toward the Project*

The ultimate goal of a strengths-based project team is to direct their collec-tive strengths toward completing their project on time, within budget, and according to the project objectives and specifications. Understanding and using the individual strengths-based building blocks and strengths-based team concepts (Chapters 3 and 4) gives a project team the foundation they need for this next step of applying their collective strengths. Chapter 6 offers strengths development and application processes for equipping your project team to intentionally apply their collective strengths.

## Strengths Development Process Overview for Strengths-Based Project Teams

Developing and becoming a strengths-based project team is a process. In order for project teams to become strengths-based project teams, project team members first need a foundation of and an engagement in *individual* strengths-based development. Individual strengths development equips each team member to discover, appreciate, and articulate their talents and strengths, discover their talents and current strengths in motion, and be intentional about personally developing and applying their talents and strengths.

Second, once each strengths-based team member can articulate and share their talent themes, dominant talents, and developed strengths with their project team, the team members can then develop an understanding and an appreciation of each of their project team members' talent themes, dominant talents, and developed strengths. In addition, each team member can communicate to their project team how they can best contribute to the team's project. The project team as a whole is then better equipped to use and leverage their collective strengths toward their project.

Exhibit 3.5 presents the process of project team strengths development. The foundation blocks will be further explored in Chapters 4 and 6.

*Note*: it is important to have a solid strengths development foundation. Without a strong foundation, your strengths-based talent development process will crumble and not be sustainable. Invest time to acquire a solid strengths development foundation before adding more strengths development building blocks to your PM tool kit.

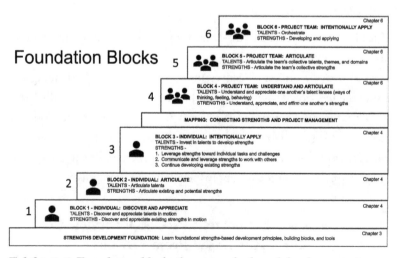

*Exhibit 3.5 Foundation blocks for strengths-based development for project teams*

# Summary

For project team members to begin the process of becoming a *strengths-based* project team, they need to have a solid foundation in individual strengths development and understand the characteristics of a strengths-based project team. Strengths begin with dominant talents. The general and specific project management knowledge, skills, and practice that you invest in your dominant talents will yield a high return on investment and help you to better contribute to your project team. Strengths-based project teams are a collection of complementary partners who maximize their collective strengths toward their project. The strengths development knowledge and skills you collect are tools that you can add to a strengths development compartment in your PM tool kit. The knowledge and tools you have collected so far will equip you to begin to engage in the process of individual strengths development (Chapter 4).

# Key Questions

1. Strengths development philosophy is founded on positive psychology—what is "right" with people rather than what is "wrong" with people. In what situations do you experience positive psychology in your workplace or on project teams?
2. What are some key strengths development take-aways for you?
3. Think of an example of one of your complementary partnerships. In what ways have you contributed your talents and strengths to this partnership? How has your complementary partner contributed their talents and strengths to your partnership?

# Notes

1. Winseman, Clifton, and Liesveld (2008, p. 7).
2. Gallup Strengths Center. 2018. https://gallupstrengthscenter.com (accessed March 24, 2018).
3. Winseman, Clifton, and Liesveld (2008, p. 7).
4. Winseman, Clifton, and Liesveld (2008, p. 8).
5. Quote from Curt Liesveld.
6. Liesveld (2014, Location 104).

7. Rath (2007, p. 20).
8. Rath (2007, p. 18).
9. Rath (2007, p. 20).
10. Clifton and Buckingham (2001, pp. 151–56).
11. PMBOK® Guide. (2013, p. 292).
12. Rath (2008).
13. Rath and Conchie (2009).
14. Darby (2012).
15. Clifton and Nelson (2010, p. 94).
16. Wagner and Muller (2009, p. 12).
17. Wagner and Muller (2009, pp. 13–14).

# References

Clifton, D.O., and M. Buckingham. 2001. *Now, Discover Your Strengths*. New York, NY: The Free Press.

Clifton, D.O., E. Anderson, and L. Schreiner. 2006. *Strengths Quest: Discover and Develop Your Strengths in Academics, Career, and Beyond*. New York, NY: Gallup Press.

Clifton, D.O., and P. Nelson. 2010. *Soar with Your Strengths*. New York, NY: Bantam Books.

Darby, R. December 12, 2012. "What is a Strengths Based Team?" *Gallup, Inc. CliftonStrengths Coaching Blog*. http://coaching.gallup.com/2012/12/what-is-strengths-based-team.html (accessed January 31, 2018).

https://gallupstrengthscenter.com (accessed January 31, 2018).

https://.gallupstrengthscenter.com/Home/en-US/CliftonStrengths-Themes-Domains (accessed January 31, 2018).

Liesveld, C. 2014. *Expanding Your Strengths*. New York, NY: Gallup Press.

PMBOK® Guide. 2013. *A Guide to the Project Management Body of Knowledge*, 5th ed. Newtown Square, PA: Project Management Institute.

Rath, T. 2007. *StrengthsFinder 2.0*. New York, NY: Gallup Press.

Rath, T., and B. Conchie. 2008. *Strengths Based Leadership*. New York, NY: Gallup Press.

Rath, T., and B. Conchie. February 3, 2009. "What Makes a Great Leadership Team?" *Gallup Inc. Business Journal*. http://businessjournal.gallup.com/content/113338/what-makes-great-leadership-team.aspx#2 (accessed January 31, 2018).

Wagner, R., and G. Muller. 2009. *Power of 2*. New York, NY: Gallup Press.

Winseman, A.L., D.O. Clifton, and C. Liesveld. 2008. *Living Your Strengths*. New York, NY: Gallup Press.

# CHAPTER 4

# Starting Point: Developing Your Strengths as a Project Manager

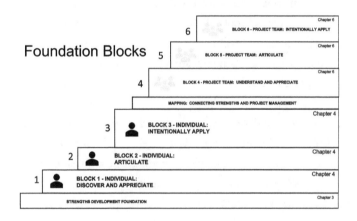

Strengths-based project teams start with the strengths of the project manager; therefore, to lead and manage a strengths-based project team, project managers need to first engage in their own individual strengths-based development. This chapter will guide you in the process of individual strengths-based development, much of which can also be applied to help project team members begin their individual strengths-based development.

Since this book is only the "tip of the iceberg" about strengths-based talent development and strengths-based project teams, we encourage you to explore the many resources available to you for more extensive and deeper individual strengths-based development information and processes. Check out the additional resources listed in Appendix A.

The purpose of this chapter is to help you:

1. Continue adding strengths development tools to your PM tool kit
2. Take the CliftonStrengths assessment

3. Use strengths development building blocks (presented in Chapter 3)
4. Discover, appreciate, and articulate your talents and strengths
5. Intentionally apply your talents and strengths
6. Use your strengths for leading and managing the project team

In Chapter 3, we presented the foundation blocks (Exhibit 3.5) for strengths development. Having started with foundational strengths-based development principles and tools (in Chapter 3), you are now ready to explore blocks 1, 2, and 3 in this chapter (Exhibit 4.1)—individual talent and strengths development.

Throughout this chapter, you will be learning about and using more strengths development tools. To fully engage in this chapter and future chapters' objectives, you will need to create a "compartment" in your PM tool kit to keep and maintain your strengths development tools. In Chapter 2, we briefly defined a PM tool kit as "a unique combination of specific project management knowledge, experiences, skills, concepts, approaches, techniques, tools, and resources that the team member has acquired, has learned to use, and continues to add to over time." Your *strengths development tools compartment* in your PM tool kit can be a physical or electronic system of keeping track of strengths development exercises and processes that you are learning to use. Your strengths development tools compartment is also a place for you to retain your responses and reflections that you write and compile as you engage in strengths development exercises and processes. Appendix B has sample templates from exercises used in the book that will also be good tools to add to your strengths development tools compartment.

We encourage you to move through each of the following strengths-based development sections before moving on to the next section. Take

## Foundation Blocks

*Exhibit 4.1  Individual talent and strengths development*

time to absorb and assimilate this information for your project environment and learning style. Most of the tools will resonate with you, even though some may be somewhat challenging. If there is an exercise or process that is very frustrating for you, it is best to put the specific exercise/process aside and come back to it at another time.

Just as talents and strengths are unique and specific for each person, how each person best engages in strengths development is also somewhat unique. As you engage in the strengths development process, you will be able to determine which strengths development tools work best for you.

## CliftonStrengths (StrengthsFinder) Assessment

Where to begin? You start with yourself. To engage in individual strengths development, you will need to take the online CliftonStrengths talent assessment. A CliftonStrengths code can be purchased in two ways:

- Online at the Gallup website (www.gallupstrengthscenter.com)
- Gallup CliftonStrengths books, such as *StrengthsFinder 2.0.*

When you purchase your code online or begin to use a code from a Gallup book, you will also be given an opportunity to set-up your own Gallup Strengths Center account (username and password), which will give you access to resources and tools for your individual strengths development after you take the CliftonStrengths assessment. Once your code is purchased, follow the instructions at the website for taking the CliftonStrengths assessment. The following instructions may also be helpful:

- We know project managers are busy. Try to find at least 45 minutes of uninterrupted time to complete the web-based talent assessment.
- You will be presented with several pairs of potential self-descriptors and will be asked to choose which descriptor best describes you, as well as the extent to which it does or does not describe you. You are allotted 20 seconds for each question before the assessment will move on to the next

question. Try not to think too hard about the questions and *give your first gut response.*

After you complete the assessment, you will be given your Clifton-Strengths Signature Themes—your top five dominant talent themes. Your top five themes give you a starting point in which to name your specific, unique talents, which are the foundations for your current and future strengths. Knowing your top five talent themes is a first step in being more intentional about using your talents and strengths when managing project teams and working with stakeholders.

Throughout this book, we will refer to your top five themes. Your top five themes are your top five dominant talent themes; however, you have more than five dominant themes. If you are interested in exploring more of your dominant talent themes, refer to the Gallup website to learn more about acquiring your 34 CliftonStrengths Theme profile.

> *STOP! At this time, we encourage you to put the book aside and take the CliftonStrengths talent assessment. Having your assessment results will make the following sections and chapters more relevant and informative.*

## Strengths Development Philosophy and Basic Building Blocks

If you purchase your CliftonStrengths assessment code at the Gallup Strengths Center website, you may have access to an electronic version of the book, *StrengthsFinder 2.0*, when you log in to your account main page. The introductory chapters of *StrengthsFinder 2.0* are a good resource for further understanding strengths development philosophy and building blocks that were presented in Chapter 3. The last part of the *Strengths-Finder 2.0* book summarizes each of the 34 CliftonStrengths Themes; however, initially it is best to focus on your own top five themes. As you engage in strengths conversations and learn about your other project team members' top five themes, you can then look back at *StrengthsFinder 2.0* to learn more about the other themes.

An additional resource for learning about the 34 CliftonStrengths Themes as aligned with project management is presented in Chapter 5 and Appendix C, which will give you another tool to add to your PM tool kit's *strengths development compartment* to further understand and apply the themes to project management.

## Discover, Appreciate, and Articulate Talents and Strengths

To fully engage in strengths development, a person first needs to be able to name their talents and strengths and see how their talents and strengths are already working in their everyday life—and on projects—before they move into the next step of intentionally applying their talents and strengths toward their current and future projects, goals, challenges, and tasks. The tools and exercises presented in this section are interrelated, interdependent, and will help you to engage in the processes of discovering, appreciating, and articulating your talents and strengths.

### CliftonStrengths Reports

Your CliftonStrengths reports list and summarize your top five talent themes. You can always find your CliftonStrengths reports by signing into the website where you took your CliftonStrengths assessment.

Your ***Signature Themes Report*** lists your top five dominant signature themes—your top five **Talent Themes**—and a *general* summary for each of your top five themes. (These general summaries are the same general summaries found in the *StrengthsFinder 2.0* book.) If you compare your *Signature Themes Report* with another person's *Signature Themes Report* who shares one of your top five talent themes, the two of you will have an identical summary of that shared theme in your reports.

You also may have access to two additional reports: Your ***Strengths Insight Report*** and ***Strengths Insight and Action-Planning Guide***. Because your top five dominant talent themes influence and complement each other, you are also given a *Strengths Insight Report,* which includes your personalized summaries for each of your top five talent themes. Each personalized theme summary considers the intensity of the theme and of your other top five themes, giving you a customized theme summary for each of your top five talent themes. Therefore, if you compared your *Strengths Insight Report* with another person's *Strengths Insight Report* who shares one of your dominant talent themes, your summaries of the shared theme will be slightly different.

The summaries in the *Strengths Insight Report* and *Strengths Insight and Action-Planning Guide* are identical. The difference between these two reports is that the *Strengths Insight and Action-Planning Guide* also includes action items and questions to help you intentionally apply and develop your talents and strengths.

*Using Your Reports:*

- Print a copy of your **Signature Themes Report.**
  - Read over your top five signature theme summaries in your *Signature Themes Report.* As you read through each theme summary, you will notice that some of the words and phrases in the summaries describe you; however, since these are general summaries, not all the words and phrases will describe you.
  - To help you name your talents, you can highlight or underline words and phrases that describe you and use those words to help you articulate your unique and specific talents that stem from each of your top five themes. The words and phrases that you highlight indicate some of your **specific talents.**
  - If you have highlighted your report in the past, consider highlighting your report again. The lifelong process of investing in talents and developing strengths often leads people to notice more of their talents; therefore, as you highlight your report again, you may notice additional talents as compared to the last time you reviewed your report.
  - Add your highlighted *Signature Themes Report* to your PM tool kit. Periodically review your talent theme summaries in your report. As you engage in lifelong strengths development, the report's summaries may help you to notice more of your talents.

- Print a copy of your *Strengths Insight and Action-Planning Guide, if you have access to this report.*
  - Read over your summaries and reflect on the following questions:
    - What do you think about these summaries? How well do the summaries describe you?
    - Are there more words and phrases that resonate with you than in your *Signature Themes Report*? What are those words and phrases?
    - What further insights about your dominant talent themes did the summaries help you to discover?
    - How do these summaries resonate with you as a member of a project team?
  - Add your *Strengths Insight and Action-Planning Guide* to your PM tool kit. You will use this report again when you engage in the application step of strengths development.

## Tabletop Name Card

You want to see and have others see your top five themes. You can make a simple tabletop name card using cardstock and a marker. Fold a sheet of cardstock in half *or* in thirds to make your tabletop name card stand upright on a table—it will look like a triangular tent. Your tabletop name card has two sides: a front and a back. Write your **first name** and your **top five talent themes** on each side:

- On the front of the card so that others can see your name and themes.
- On the back of the card so that you can see your own themes which will help you to learn and remember your top five themes.

Place your tabletop name card on your desk, carry it with you to meetings, and use it as you engage in one-to-one strengths conversations.

**Strengths Building Blocks Lists** (Your specific talents, knowledge, skills, experiences, and strengths lists).

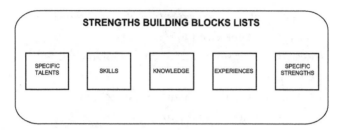

*Exhibit 4.2  Strengths building blocks lists*

In Chapter 3, we defined talents, knowledge (factual/conceptual), experiences, and skills and explained that these are the major components for building strengths. As you begin being more intentional about building your strengths, create and maintain lists for each of your specific talents, knowledge, experiences, skills, and specific strengths and keep the lists in your PM tool kit (Exhibit 4.2).

Where to begin? Here are some ways to get started on your lists:

- You have just highlighted words and phrases—your specific talents—in your Signature Themes Report. Keep track of those specific talents that you identified on your **Specific Talents List**.
- You have already started your **Specific Strengths List**. Remember in Chapter 1, you wrote down three things that you do consistently well. Use the three things you listed to start your **Specific Strengths List**.
- Take some time to think about and list the general skills, knowledge, and experiences that you have acquired over your lifetime.
- In addition, think about the specific project management conceptual knowledge, skills, and experiences that you have acquired and list those. Also list your areas of expertise.

The **Strengths Building Blocks Lists** (Exhibit 4.3) you are making are brainstorming lists: there is no specific order to the content you are adding, and there may or may not be any connection between the items in each list or between lists. Freely think about the specific knowledge,

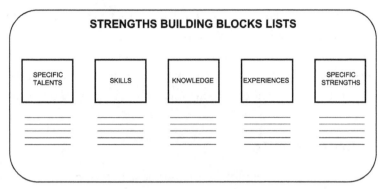

*Exhibit 4.3  Working document for your Strengths Building Blocks Lists*

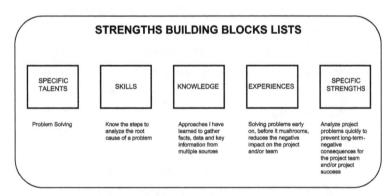

*Exhibit 4.4  Strengths building blocks lists (project management example)*

skills, and experiences you have acquired over your lifetime, the specific talents you were born with, and the things that you do consistently well right now (your current strengths).

Here is a specific project management example using the working document template (Exhibit 4.4):

As you enter into the next processes and exercises in this section and chapter, you will use and add more to your **Strengths Building Blocks Lists**. Keep your **Strengths Building Blocks Lists** in the strengths development compartment of your PM tool kit. Later, you will intentionally use some of your list's content to help you articulate how you developed your existing strengths and how you want to intentionally further develop your strengths.

What if you are not a "list" person? Use this list process to get started. Then as you engage in the process, you may develop a better system to keep track of your specific talents, knowledge, skills, experiences, and specific strengths. This is part of the creativity we discussed earlier about tailoring this book's approaches and information to fit your needs and style.

### A Talent Theme a Day

- Choose one of your top five dominant talent themes.
  - *The First Day*: As you go through your day, notice how you naturally use the talents from that theme. At the end of the day, write down the specific talents within this theme that you used during the day.
  - *The Next Couple of Days*: Find two ways to intentionally leverage the specific talents (that you named yesterday) to complete some of your assigned deliverables or tasks today. Continue this process for a few days—strengthening your ability to use talents from the theme you chose on the first day.
  - *Add to your* **Strengths Building Blocks Lists**: Add the specific talents you named and ways you used these talents to your **Specific Talents List** (one of your **Strengths Building Blocks Lists**) that you keep in the strengths development compartment of your PM tool kit.
- *Repeat the Process*: In a few days, start this step-by-step process with another one of your dominant talent themes.

When you practice using your talents in the "a talent theme a day" process, you are investing in your talents and developing your strengths by gaining experiential knowledge, one of the ingredients for developing a strength.

Keep track of what you learn from the "a talent theme a day" process, because the specific talents you name and the ways in which you use them will also help you to further engage in a subsequent strengths development step of intentionally applying your talents and strengths.

### Holding-Up the Mirror[1]

Our dominant talents are such a natural part of who we are, that sometimes we don't see them and/or appreciate their value. People who know us well can often see our talents and their value better than we can. Share your top five talent themes with a person who knows you well. This might be someone on your project team, your project sponsor, a colleague, or someone outside the project.

Take this learning opportunity to describe your top five talent themes to this person, and then ask them to tell you where he or she has seen your talents from these themes working in your life. Take some notes about the insights you gain from this conversation and consider adding what you learn to your **Strengths Building Blocks Lists**.

### Strengths Conversations

The holding-up the mirror activity is one form of a strengths conversation. Since people don't develop and use their talents and strengths in isolation, you need your project team members—and your team members need you—to fully engage in strengths development. Strengths conversations are tools and practices that you and your team members can use to help one another engage in strengths development. Strengths conversations are simply conversations around talents and strengths, which equip people to better articulate their talents, invest in their talents, further develop their current strengths, and apply their strengths.

With whom can you engage in strengths conversations? Everyone! At work, at home, in your community. Even with people who don't know about strengths development, strengths conversations give you the opportunity to tell them about talents and strengths. That said, strengths conversations will be easier to have with people who have at least a general strengths development background. Therefore, equipping your project team with the basics of strengths development will equip you and the project team to better engage in strengths conversations. As you take the initial steps for engaging in your own individual strengths development, first engage in strengths conversations with your functional manager and your peers.

Where at work can you engage in strengths conversations? In all contexts. Once your project team members understand strength development, you will be able to weave strengths conversations into your project team meetings, project status meetings, one-on-one meetings and conversations with your project team members or project sponsor, and casually at lunch or during a break.

The time commitment for strengths conversations vary, especially as individuals, teams, and organizations begin strengths development. However, once a strengths-based project team and/or organizational culture is established, strengths conversations can be effective in as little as just a few minutes.

Looking ahead: Why are strengths conversations essential for strengths-based project teams? Strengths conversations are key for maximizing the application of your own strengths and the collective strengths of your project team members and instrumental for making effective project team decisions. For example, on the project team, who has the strength(s) to best lead or complete a particular deliverable or major task? How can the project team best approach one of their specific project team challenges?

As you prepare to best maximize the collective strengths of your team, it is essential that you communicate your talents and strengths to your project team, what you need, what motivates you, what you like and don't like, and how you can best lead the project team. In turn, you need to understand the talents and strengths of your project team members, what your team members need, what motivates them, what they like and don't like, and how they can best contribute to the project team. In subsequent chapters, we will further expand upon how to practice strengths conversations with your project team.

### Strengths Partnership

Having a strengths partner will help you to engage in strengths conversations about your own and your partner's talents and strengths. Find a partner who is also interested in strengths development. Try to meet with your strengths partner once or twice a week for 20 minutes for a strengths conversation. Your strengths conversations can be simple, such as sharing your discoveries and insights from the individual strengths development exercises and processes listed in this chapter. You can also use strengths conversational ideas and prompts found in Appendix D.

### Talents and Strengths Grid (Articulating Talents and Strengths)

As you discover and articulate your talents and strengths, keep track of them in a **Talents and Strengths Grid** (Exhibit 4.5). You will also use this grid later in the strengths application step.

The following steps will help you complete the grid for your talents and strengths.

*Step One*: **Dedicate a row of the grid to each of your *existing strengths*** and list each of your current strengths in a box in the column marked "Strength: My Specific Strength." See Exhibit 4.6. (When you are finished, each box under "strength" will contain one of your current strengths.) Remember, a strength is something that you do consistently well. To get you started, fill out the first three "strengths" boxes (in the

*Exhibit 4.5 My talents and strengths grid: template*

| Talent theme | Talent | + Investment: | Skills Experience Knowledge Practice | = Strength | Ways I use/ could use this specific strength |
|---|---|---|---|---|---|
| | My specific talent | My specific talent investments | | My specific strength | |
| | | | | | |
| | | | | | |
| | | | | | |
| | | | | | |
| | | | | | |

*Exhibit 4.6 My talents and strengths grid: Specific strength*

| Talent theme | Talent | + Investment: | Skills Experience Knowledge Practice | = Strength | Ways I use/could use this specific strength |
|---|---|---|---|---|---|
| | My specific talent | My specific talent investments | | My specific strength | |
| | | | | My strength is my ability to collect and share relevant data with the project team | |

column marked "My Specific Strength") with the strengths that you listed in Chapter 1.

*Step Two*: Also **dedicate a row of your grid to each of your *specific talents*** and list each of your specific talents in a box in the column marked "Talent: My Specific Talent." (Each box under "Talent" will contain one of your natural talents.) Remember, a talent is a way that you naturally think, feel, or behave. Use your highlighted *Signature Themes Report* to get you started. The words you highlighted are descriptors of your talents.

If you use your report to articulate your talents, you will also be able to list the talent theme that your specific talent is anchored in. Put the name of the theme in the column next to the "Talent: My Specific Talent," as shown in Exhibit 4.7.

If you articulate some of your specific talents without using your report (articulating your talents "organically"), you still have the option of including the talent theme you think your specific talent is anchored in; however, you do not have to write down a talent theme in the respective row. On the other hand, feel free to write down more than one talent theme if you see your specific talent anchored in more than one talent theme.

For now, you can leave the "Investment" column blank (Exhibit 4.8). The grid's purpose now is to help you to create a list of your specific

*Exhibit 4.7 My talents and strengths grid: Talent theme with specific talent*

| Talent theme | Talent | + Investment: | Skills Experience Knowledge Practice | = Strength | Ways I use/ could use this specific strength |
|---|---|---|---|---|---|
| | My specific talent | My specific talent investments | | My specific strength | |
| Input® | I enjoy gathering and sharing information. I am a collector of resources | | | My strength is my ability to collect and share relevant data with the project team | |

talents and strengths, which you can intentionally use later when you engage in the application step of strengths development.

This grid is for you. There is no right or wrong way to use this grid. The instructions listed here are to get you started. As you use this grid,

*Exhibit 4.8 My talents and strengths grid: Investments (blank)*

| Talent theme | Talent | + Investment: | Skills Experience Knowledge Practice | = Strength | Ways I use/ could use this specific strength |
|---|---|---|---|---|---|
| | My specific talent | My specific talent investments | | My specific strength | |
| Input® | I enjoy gathering and sharing information. I am a collector of resources | | | My strength is my ability to collect and share relevant data with the project team | |

you may develop new approaches to keeping track of your specific talents and specific strengths.

Give the grid a try. It is a terrific tool for organizing, tracking, and showing progress! We will be referring back to this grid later in this chapter. As you move forward in strengths development, continue to add to and refer to your **Talents and Strengths Grid**.

## Intentionally Apply Talents and Strengths

Since you have discovered, appreciated, and articulated your talents and strengths, you are ready to engage in the *application* of your talents and strengths. Often, people skip the strengths-development "application" component because it can be challenging; however, just like discovering, appreciating, and articulating your talents are essential components of strengths development, intentionally applying your talents and strengths is also essential! Strengths-based development is more than just knowing about your talents and strengths—it's also about maximizing and using your talents and strengths in your role as you work with others, including working with your project team members.

In Chapter 3, we explained key purposes for intentionally applying talents and strengths:

- Invest in talents to develop strengths
- Leverage strengths
- Continue developing existing strengths

The following application exercises will help you to begin being intentional about applying your talents and strengths. Although the exercises are presented in connection with the key application purposes, the exercises are also interrelated.

### Invest in Talents to Develop Strengths

The following two exercises will guide you in the process of being more intentional about investing in your specific talents.

### Strengths Insight and Action-Planning Guide (CliftonStrengths Report)

1. Look over your *Strengths Insight and Action-Planning Guide, if you have access to this report.*
2. In the "Awareness" section, read your customized talent theme summaries again and reflect on the section's questions.
3. In the "Application" section, you will find a list of action items connected to each of your top five talent themes.
    (a) Choose one or two specific action items from *one* talent theme to help you invest in your talents and develop your strengths.
        i. Focus on your chosen action item(s) for a few days.
        ii. Take some notes about your experience with each action item.
        iii. Can you add more insights to your strengths building blocks lists? To your talents and strengths grid?
    (b) After a few days, choose an action item(s) from another talent theme.

### Talents and Strengths Grid

Your talents and strengths grid can help you keep track of your ideas for developing your talent potential and ways that you have already successfully invested in your specific talents.

1. Pull out your **Talents and Strengths Grid**. Designate a new row on your grid for this exercise.
2. Look at your specific talents that you have articulated so far in the "Talents: My Specific Talents" column on your **Talents and Strengths Grid**. Also look at your **Specific Talents List** you have made.
3. Choose one of your specific talents and insert the specific talent in a new row on the grid.
4. Is there a potential strength that you would like to develop from the specific talent you chose? Articulate and include the strength that you want to develop in the same row as the specific talent you just included in your grid.

5. What are some ways that you would use that strength? Include your insights in your grid under "Ways I use/could use this specific strength."

6. Brainstorm ways you could invest in your specific talent to get to the strength you would like to develop. Under the "investment section" of your grid, include your insights in the same row to which you just added the specific strength that you want to develop.

7. You are using your grid to articulate ways that you *could be* intentional about investing in your talents to develop your strengths. Create a *Developing Strengths Action Plan* to keep track of the ways that you *will* invest in your talents.

Exhibit 4.9 gives you an example of what a partially completed grid might look like.

After you use your grid to name specific ways that you could invest in your talent to develop a strength, consider color-coding or creating a system for your grid which would indicate strengths you have developed and strengths you are currently developing. Remember, this grid is yours—how you develop and use this grid will be unique for you.

Your grid will help you to articulate the several elements that can come together over time to form a strength: What goes into a strength? How can I develop this strength?

Here is another specific project management example and template for developing and/or articulating a strength. All project managers need to be able to communicate well. In this example, a project manager has combined his unique, *specific talent(s)* with his acquired skills, knowledge, experiences, and project management tools, techniques, and/or core competencies to develop a strength to be able to communicate well. He describes his **specific strength** as having the ability to "**consistently communicate well what stakeholders need to know**."

This project manager *does not* have dominant Communication® talents; however, he chose to invest in one of his dominant, **specific talents**—his natural "**interest and inclination to ask questions to learn about what others are thinking**"—to develop the ability to "**consistently communicate well what stakeholders need to know**"—his **specific strength**.

Exhibit 4.9 *My talents and strengths grid: Completed example*

| Talent theme | Talent | + Investment: Skills Experience Knowledge Practice | = Strength | Ways I use/could use this specific strength |
|---|---|---|---|---|
| | My specific talent | My specific talent investments | My specific strength | |
| Input® | I enjoy gathering and sharing information. I am a collector of resources | **Skills:** I want to invest in a step-by-step process to quickly organize all the data that I have collected<br><br>**Conceptual Knowledge:** Become proficient in questioning techniques, critical thinking, and researching methods<br><br>**Practice:** Ensure that the "things" (data, information, articles, books, etc.) I collect have purpose— to be useful to myself and others. Practice being aware that just because I crave more knowledge, doesn't mean that others do. Be inquisitive. Use caution not to download too much data during high-level discussions (such as at project Kickoff meetings)<br><br>*Further invest-in/develop strength:*<br>**Experience:** Acquire experience to effectively and efficiently "sift" through volumes of information to easily locate relevant data | My strength is my ability to collect and share relevant data with the project team | I use this strength by being an inquirer: I ask questions, probe for evidence-based answers, and seek information from others working on the project |

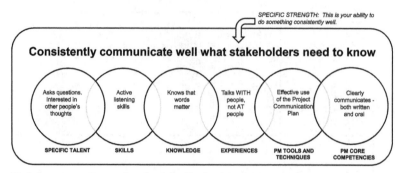

*Exhibit 4.10 Example of strengths building blocks lists*

His peers may also have developed specific strengths for being an excellent communicator but *how* they develop their strengths and how they *articulate* their specific "excellent communicator" strengths will vary depending on what their specific talents are.

Exhibit 4.10 shows how the project manager in our previous example invested in his specific talent over time to develop his specific strength.

Just like the talent and strength grid is unique to you, the "circles" or elements that make up your strength will also be unique to you.

## Leverage Strengths Toward Tasks and Challenges

How can you best use your strengths? As an individual? As a project manager? And a project team member? Consider these four steps to get started:

1. Make a list of your tasks and challenges:
   (a) What tasks are you currently responsible for?
   (b) What challenges are you facing right now?
2. Choose one task or challenge.
3. Using your **Strengths Building Blocks Lists** and your **Talents and Strengths Grid**, think about what strengths you can leverage toward your chosen task or challenge.
   (a) Which of your strengths do you think you could leverage in this situation?
   (b) Have you used a specific strength toward a similar task or challenge in the past? Did using that strength result in success? Could you leverage this strength in this situation?

(c) Is there a person with complementary strengths who you could partner with as you leverage your strengths in this situation?

4. You are articulating ways that you *could be* intentional about leveraging your strengths. Create a *Professional Development Plan* for how you plan to complete the task or approach the challenge, including ways that you can use some of your specific strengths. (You will find a template for a *Professional Development Plan* in Appendix B.)

By creating your *Professional Development Plan*, you will now have a roadmap to guide you in intentionally applying your strengths. In Chapter 8, you will learn more about using a *Professional Development Plan*.

## Leverage Your Strengths to Work with Others

The effect of using your strengths grows exponentially when you leverage your strengths in collaboration with others.[2] How can you get started leveraging your strengths in collaboration with others on a project team? Here are some first steps:

1. **Post Your Top Five Talent Themes** near your desk (e.g., table top name card you made earlier), in your email signature block, or on the project team's virtual "white board."
2. **Engage in Strengths Conversations** with your functional manager, your peers/colleagues, and other team members.
3. **Form Complementary Partnerships** with your colleagues and project team members.
4. **Look for Talents and Strengths in Motion** from your colleagues and project team members. When you see one of your colleagues or project team members using their talents and strengths, tell them! It can be a simple note that you leave on their desk or a simple verbal accolade. If you are working on a global project team, consider the different country cultures for sharing this information. The benefits of looking for talents and strengths in motion include:
   (a) Injects positivity into your workplace
   (b) Lets your colleagues and project team members know that you noticed their good work

(c) Holds-up the mirror for your project team members—they may not be aware of the talents and strengths that they have

(d) Promotes strengths conversations on the project team

(e) Affirms and sustains a strengths-based project team culture

(f) Celebrates the successes of the project team—no matter how small

## Continue Developing Existing Strengths

As you continue to discover and articulate your current strengths, add your strengths and how you developed them to your **Talents and Strengths Grid** and your **Strengths Building Blocks Lists**. Identifying your existing strengths and then how you developed those strengths will help you to further develop your current strengths.

1. Choose one of your current strengths (from your grid or lists).
2. If you have not done so, use your grid to write down ways that you already use this strength.
3. Try to name and add to your grid a specific talent and its respective talent theme that you invested in (intentionally or unintentionally) to develop this specific strength.
4. What specific skills, knowledge, and experiences did you acquire to develop that specific strength? Add those to your grid.
5. Think about and articulate ways that you could further develop this specific strength. Add these ideas to your grid.
6. Use your *Developing Strengths Action Plan* to keep track of the ways that you *will* continue to develop your existing strengths.

## Use Your Strengths to Lead and Manage the Project Team

As a project manager, it is your role to lead and manage the project team. How you can best fulfill your specific project manager role depends on your talents and strengths; therefore, it is to your advantage to consider and articulate specific ways to leverage your strengths as you lead and manage your team.

How can you be more intentional about leveraging your strengths in your project manager role? You have already practiced using some processes for intentionally applying your talents and strengths. You have started a *Professional Development Plan* and created a *Developing Strengths Action Plan*. Now, you can maximize the talents and strengths application process to dive deeper into your specific project management strengths and the strengths you want to further develop:

1. Articulate three of your tasks or challenges that you have in your project manager role.
2. Pull out your **Strengths Building Blocks Lists** and **Talents and Strengths Grid.** Think about ways in which you could apply your strengths toward each of the three tasks or challenges you named. List your ideas.
3. Are there strengths that you could also develop or further develop to leverage toward your chosen tasks or challenges?
   (a)  What specific strength do you want to develop? What specific talent(s) would this strength be anchored in?
   (b)  What additional project management tools do you need to acquire to develop the strength you identified earlier?
       i.  What trainings could you attend?
       ii.  How can you practice and apply what you learn in training to gain experience for further developing your strength?
4. Articulate one or two action items for applying your strengths to your tasks or challenges and include in your *Professional Development Plan*. If you have specific strengths to develop, include how you will develop those strengths in your *Developing Strengths Action Plan*.

Give yourself time to "experiment" with this process of intentionally investing your project management knowledge, skills, and experiences into your talents and strengths.

Keep in mind that the strengths you develop from acquiring specific project management knowledge, techniques, and tools may look different compared to another project manager who acquires the same knowledge, techniques, and tools. How each of you best carries out your role as a project manager will vary depending on your talents and strengths even with the same tool kit. In addition, you are each working on different projects and with different team members with different talents and strengths. Therefore, in addition to learning from other project managers, be sure to experiment with the strengths you have developed in your various project management roles and use your unique strengths to maximize your effectiveness and success as a project manager.

## Summary

Strengths-based project team development begins with the project manager's individual strengths development. The best strengths development "storage" are compartments in your PM tool kit where you can keep and maintain your strengths development tools plus track your progress and reflections. Start by taking the CliftonStrengths assessment to obtain your top five dominant talent themes. After taking the assessment, continually use the information in your CliftonStrengths reports to further develop your strengths.

Leverage the exercises presented in this chapter for your individual strengths development. Use your knowledge of strengths development building blocks to discover, appreciate, articulate, and apply your talents and strengths. Strengths-based development is knowing, maximizing, and using your talents and strengths in your role on a project team. The strengths development tools you have added to your PM tool kit prepares you to begin to guide your project team members in individual and project team strengths development. It starts with you!

## Key Questions

1. What was your first impression of your top five talent themes in your *Signature Themes Report*?
   a. Did any part of your report surprise you?
   b. Did you discover any new ways to articulate your talents?
   c. Is there any part of the report that you have questions about?
2. *You have articulated* some of your **strengths** through the exercises in this chapter. Look over your list and then answer the following questions:

   a. What do you like about being able to apply your strengths in your project manager role? What about the application process do you want to learn more about and practice?

   b. Give an example of how you currently use one of your strengths in your current project management role. Then think about and articulate ways that you could use your other strengths in your current project management role.

3. How can using the talents and strengths grid benefit you? Then think about your project team: How could your project team benefit if each team member uses the grid?

## Notes

1. Winseman, Clifton, and Liesveld (2008, p. 23).
2. Winseman, Clifton, and Liesveld (2008, p. 27).

## References

PMBOK® Guide. 2017. *A Guide to the Project Management Body of Knowledge*, 6th ed. Newtown Square, PA: Project Management Institute.

Winseman, A.L., D.O. Clifton, and C. Liesveld. 2008. *Living Your Strengths*. New York, NY: Gallup Press.

# CHAPTER 5

# Mapping: Connecting Strengths and Project Management

In Chapters 3 and 4, you were introduced to strengths-based talent development philosophy and building blocks and learned approaches for your own individual strengths-based development. This chapter takes a deeper look at each of the 34 CliftonStrengths Themes though the lens of project management to equip you to better articulate and invest in your talents toward *project management strengths*.

The purpose of this chapter is to:

1. Connect the CliftonStrengths Themes to project management
2. Explain "theme dynamics" using a project management connection map
3. Explore how theme dynamics can impact developing project management strengths

## A PM Connection Map for Using CliftonStrengths Themes in Project Management

Meet Timothy Kloppenborg. Tim is a trainer, consultant, distinguished professor emeritus, author, and editor. More importantly, he is a certified Project Management Professional (PMP®) by the Project Management Institute and has been trained as a strengths development coach by the Gallup organization to help teams develop their collective strengths.

Tim has connected the 34 CliftonStrengths Themes to project management by writing a brief summary for each theme through the lens of project management, giving project team members a *project management connection map* to guide them as they intentionally apply their talents to project management. With written permission from South-Western, a part of Cengage, Inc., we are sharing this map with you (Exhibit 5.1). For ease of reference, Tim's theme summaries, as shown in the following, also appear in Appendix C.

*Exhibit 5.1*[1] *Connecting talent themes to project management*

## Strengths Themes as Used in Project Management*

*All theme names are trademarked by Gallup, Inc.

### Achiever®

You must accomplish something every day. You have great stamina and internal motivation. When you finish one task, you quickly want to work on another so you can complete milestones. You manage proactively by setting plans, working to achieve them, and asking people to report progress.

### Activator®

You want to make decisions and start quickly. Results of early actions will provide input into following decisions and actions. You want to be judged by your actions and results. You encourage others to action and help them overcome obstacles. You create a sense of urgency and energy when needed.

### Adaptability®

You live in the moment. Decisions made now create the future. You keep making progress in the face of unknowns. You balance conflicting demands of tasks and people, of various stakeholders, of risks, and of proposed changes. You understand reality, bring emotional stability, and do not need to control everything.

### Analytical®

You are objective, search for reasons, and want to see proof. You ask questions, research intensively, and then develop logical explanations. In ambiguous situations, you simplify concepts, recognize patterns, understand limits, describe causes and effects, and establish order. You fearlessly make honest decisions based upon facts.

### Arranger®

You are organized, yet flexible. You have defined values and priorities. You arrange people and other resources, improving work processes to best achieve your primary objectives. You thrive on cooperation and collaboration in complex settings. You depend on honest, timely, and transparent information to make rapid adjustments.

### Belief®

You possess enduring core values that guide and energize your behavior. You walk the talk as a dependable and trustworthy sounding board. You are committed to work and people, encouraging your team to display high ethics and to help others.

### Command®

You take charge, directly sharing your opinions and aligning people to your goals. You challenge others and lead forcefully when necessary. You thrive in crisis, making rapid decisions and encouraging others to take risks.

### Communication®

You speak and write clearly. You place high value on human interaction, talking with—not to—people. You tell stories to enliven your ideas, gain commitment, and maintain enthusiasm. You ask good questions, listen well, and help others express their feelings. You "think out loud" and encourage collaboration.

### Competition®

You want to outperform everyone either individually or as a team. This invigorates you and helps you achieve your ambitions. You define, measure, and ensure progress. You select contests you believe you can win and then celebrate your successes.

### Connectedness®

You believe everything happens for a reason and is part of something larger. Your thinking extends beyond your self-interests. You see no boundaries and celebrate when people find common ground around shared meaning. Your hopefulness helps you achieve personal and organizational goals.

### Consistency®

You treat everyone the same, with clear rules based upon values. You create a predictable and calm environment. You value loyalty and routines and accurately document requirements.

### Context®

You look back to understand the original purpose and past actions that shaped the present. You share stories to connect with people. You ask questions and take time to understand root causes. This perspective gives you confidence to decide what is enduring and what can change, inspiring confidence in followers.

### Deliberative®

You are a private person who identifies and analyzes risks, plans carefully, avoids problems, trusts your instincts, and makes no hasty decisions. You help others consider all factors in sensitive decisions. You have a few close friends in whom you confide. You only praise when it is well deserved.

### Developer®

You see potential and small improvements in people. You enjoy observing, advising, encouraging, challenging, and improving inexperienced people. You encourage teams to try, fail, and try again, helping them set appropriate expectations and celebrate success. By mentoring individuals, you develop effective teams.

### Discipline®

The world can be chaotic, but you create predictability with plans, priorities, routines, timelines, and structures. Through your attention to detailed planning and consistent execution, you create order and deliver effective and timely results. You carefully monitor progress, adhere to uncompromising standards, and celebrate excellence.

### Empathy®

You are highly instinctive and feel the emotions of others so strongly, it is as if they were your own. You do not necessarily agree with others' choices, but you understand. You respect everyone's feelings and help them express them. People trust your discretion and you help resolve conflict.

### Focus®

You work best when you know what is important and have a clear end goal. You define outcomes, determine priorities, set intermediate goals, follow through, make mid-course corrections, and deliver results. You concentrate deeply and are impatient with delays. You help others set goals and concentrate on critical issues.

### Futuristic®

You are intrigued by the future and enjoy describing your conceptions of it. Your emotional yet realistic contemplations help others to understand how supporting your project helps them accomplish their goals.

### Harmony®

You look for a common ground to find agreement. You value expert perspectives, perhaps merging ideas as long as you retain your basic values and shared sense of purpose. You have a calm, facilitating manner, avoid confrontation, bring practical knowledge, and strive for consensus.

### Ideation®

You are energized by finding new perspectives on familiar situations. You are innovative and creative, love to brainstorm, and strive to make things better. You take calculated risks and share excitement. You create useful plans, overcoming resource limits and risks.

### Includer®

You feel the pain of those who are left out and understand the power of a larger team of active and unified participants in which all voices are heard. You are accepting, as you feel we are all equally important. You ensure information and decision making are widely shared.

### Individualization®

You perceive differences in how people think, feel, and behave. You bring out the best in each person and foster effective, diverse teams in which everyone is encouraged to do what they do best. As a mentor and leader, you treat each person according to their unique needs and dreams.

### Input®

Your curiosity enables you to be a great researcher. You enjoy being up to date and gathering and sharing information. You view whatever you collect—ideas or tangible items—as resources. You may be an expert or good at making concepts seem real.

### Intellection®

You enjoy taking quiet time to read and think. While your thoughts may be focused or diverse, you often generate wisdom and clarity. You help your team make better decisions by asking great questions, giving your honest opinions, and engaging in deep conversations.

### Learner®

You are energized by the process of learning and considering possibilities. You excel on short project assignments and as a change agent where you need to learn quickly. As you continuously study and improve, you gain confidence. You help your team improve by co-learning with them and tracking lessons learned.

### Maximizer®

Your greatest joy is taking good performance of your own, of another individual, or of a team to a higher level. You prefer to capitalize upon raw talent. You strive for quality and excellence.

### Positivity®

You always see and communicate the good. You lift others with your enthusiasm. Life and work are fun. You give people frequent praise and focus on making progress no matter the situation. Your hope for the future, good humor, and eagerness to celebrate make you a valued team member.

### Relator®

You enjoy being around your close friends, learning about their feelings and goals. You derive satisfaction from working hard with these friends. You honor trust and show respect.

### Responsibility®

You enjoy volunteering, and when you commit, no one needs to check your progress. You have the highest ethics, usually fulfilling your many obligations, and making amends when you cannot. You are a serious, dedicated role model. You may feel overwhelmed, but you are satisfied when you complete commitments.

### Restorative™

You diagnose problems, determine root causes, and implement solutions. Bad news with no sugar coating motivates you, whether it concerns people or things. You can identify risks and devise contingency plans in advance.

### Self-Assurance®

Your confidence inspires others. You research issues and listen to experts, but then make up your own mind and act decisively. You completely commit to critical challenges not because you have no fear, but because you know someone needs to lead and you are bold and resolute.

### Significance®

You want to make a lasting difference in this world and be known for it. You dream big dreams, need affirmation, fear failure, but are comfortable with risk and public scrutiny. You champion others' needs and achievements. You want to associate with other top performers.

### Strategic®

You plan backward from goals to various means of accomplishing them. You see patterns where others see chaos. You research alternatives and select one—often avoiding potential problems. You see the big picture and are flexible concerning how to achieve it.

### Woo®

You enjoy meeting new people and discovering common interests or other connections. The thrill of meeting a new person may be greater than developing a deep relationship. You naturally put people at ease and facilitate interchange of ideas. You ask questions and get others to support your goals.

The preceding project management connection map is an excellent resource for your PM tool kit. Not only does it help you begin to understand your own talent themes as you apply your talents and strengths in managing projects, but Tim's talent theme descriptions can also help you to understand the themes of other key individuals associated with the project—project team members, stakeholders, and the project sponsor.

The previous summary descriptions indicate talents often stemming from each of the respective themes. Here are some examples of specific talents taken directly from Tim's summaries:

- "Treat each person according to their unique needs" (Individualization®)
- Driven to "diagnose problems" (Restorative™)
- "Eagerness to celebrate" (Positivity®)
- Desire to "simplify concepts" (Analytical®)
- "Enjoy meeting new people," such as stakeholders (WOO®)
- "Feel the emotions of others" (Empathy®)
- "Energized by the process of learning" (Learner®)
- "Have great stamina and internal motivation" (Achiever®)
- "See …the potential in people" (Developer®)
- Naturally "take charge" (Command®)
- "Encourage others to action" (Activator®)
- "Enjoys … gathering and sharing information" (Input®)

Now that you see the connection between project management and the different talent themes, consider doing the following exercise—individually and later as a project team.

## Exercise

Step 1: Take a look at Exhibit 5.1.
Step 2: Find your top five CliftonStrengths Themes and read the project management summary description.
Step 3: Reflect on how these descriptions resonate with you.
***Later, as you read and do exercises in Chapter 6, come back to this exercise to do Steps 4 and 5.***

Step 4: Read about your fellow team members' top five talent themes in Exhibit 5.1.

Step 5: Have a strengths-based conversation as a project team about the theme descriptions from Exhibit 5.1:

- Invite project team members to share with the team how their own top five theme descriptions from Exhibit 5.1 resonate with them or do not resonate with them.
- Ask team members to give an example of how they have used talents—described in Exhibit 5.1's theme descriptions—on a project team.
- Encourage team members to suggest other words or phrases that describe talents from their own top five themes—words and phrases that are not listed in Exhibit 5.1's theme descriptions.

In Chapter 6, you will learn about applying Chapters 3, 4, and 5 to your project team. The aforementioned project team exercise can be extremely beneficial in the process of accelerating an "ordinary" project team in becoming an "extraordinary" strengths-based project team, because the exercise helps the project manager and project team members to more quickly and deeply understand, appreciate, and articulate the project team members' talents. This exercise is also a foundational exercise for equipping the project team to later apply their collective strengths toward their project.

## Theme Dynamics—What Is It?

Considering ways in which each talent theme connects to project management will help your project team members to further articulate and apply their talents and strengths. As you see the potential of talents from each of the talent themes specifically for project management, also keep in mind that a person's dominant talent themes work together and influence each other. For example:

Team Member A has the following top five talent themes:

- Achiever®
- Focus®

- Harmony®
- Input®
- Maximizer®

Team Member B has the following top five talent themes:

- Achiever®
- Analytical®
- Arranger®
- Relator®
- Responsibility®

Notice that both team members have one talent theme in common—Achiever®; their other four top talent themes are different. Since their specific talents from each of their other four themes influence their Achiever® talents, Team Member A's Achiever® talents and strengths will be slightly different than Team Member B's Achiever® talents and strengths. While both team members could be "driven" to get something done every day and get results, how, why, and to what end they are driven will be somewhat nuanced due to their other themes. For example:

- Team Member A's drive to get things done is influenced by her Focus® talents, which she uses to manage distractions that could get in the way. While Team Member B's drive to get things done may be influenced by his Responsibility® talents—he may be driven to get things done to fulfill the commitments he has made to others.
- Team Member A might get things done by first looking over resources she has collected and been saving or gathering ideas from others, since Input® is one of her other top five themes. While Team Member B might prefer getting things done by specifically gathering and analyzing data and facts before taking steps to get things done because Analytical® is one of his other themes.

It is the combination of talents from all of your dominant talent themes that provide you with the foundation for your strengths. Talents from each of your dominant talent themes influence, affect, "enhance, modify, [and] regulate"[2] each other, which is called **theme dynamics**.[3] At times your dominant talent themes seem to complement each other, and other times, your talents might seem to be conflicting with each other. Consider how your talents complement each other, how they are different, and how they can best work together to maximize your talents' potential.

## Applying a PM Connection Map and Theme Dynamics to Strengths-Based Project Teams

Now that we have introduced theme summaries through the lens of project management and theme dynamics, let us combine and apply these two tools together for developing strengths-based project team strengths.

In Chapter 3, we explained that we can creatively leverage strengths in situations where it appears that lesser talents are needed. We then gave an example about a project team member who leveraged her strengths. The project team member in our example needs to influence her team to get things done on time, but she doesn't seem to have any dominant talents to help her to influence others.

Here is some more information about this project team member. Among her top five talent themes are Achiever®, Discipline®, and Harmony®. She has articulated her specific talents by using her *Clifton-Strengths Signature Themes Report*. She also used "Strengths Themes as Used in Project Management" (Exhibit 5.1) as a project management connection map to help her articulate ways that her specific talents from three of her dominant talent themes—Achiever®, Discipline®, and Harmony®—might connect to project management.

One of her dominant and specific **talents** that she has articulated is her *"drive to get things done efficiently."* She attributes this specific talent to her Achiever® and Discipline® themes. She has developed a **strength** rooted in her Achiever® and Discipline® themes for *"systematically keeping track of what needs to get done and checking it off her list."*

| Talent Themes: Achiever® and Discipline® |
| :--- |
| **Specific Talent:** Drive to get things done efficiently |
| **Strength:** Systematically keeping track of what needs to get done and checking it off her list |

She invested project management tools into her specific talent to develop her strength, such as monitoring progress of each task on the project schedule until each task is completed. Remember that strengths-based "investment" is investing specific knowledge, skills, and experiences into a specific talent(s) to develop a strength (Chapters 3 and 4). Project managers and project team members can also invest specific project management tools and techniques into their talents to develop strengths to use in managing projects.

| |
|---|
| **Talent Themes:** Achiever® and Discipline® |
| **Specific Talent:** Drive to get things done efficiently |
| **Investment:** Develop a simple, step-by step tracking system such as using a Kanban board |
| **Strength:** Systematically keeping track of what needs to get done and checking it off her list |

In Chapter 3, we explained that a person can creatively leverage strengths in situations where it appears that they have to use their lesser talents. We suggested that she could leverage her Achiever® and Discipline® related strength to create action items assigned in project team meetings, post the action items in a place that is accessible to all project team members, communicate where the action items are posted, and then create a system for marking each action item complete. In this way, she could leverage this strength—founded on her "driven to get things done efficiently" talent from the Achiever® and Discipline® talent themes—to *influence* her team members to get things done on time.

| |
|---|
| **Talent Themes:** Achiever® and Discipline® |
| **Specific Talent:** Drive to get things done efficiently |
| **Investment:** Become proficient in showing others how to use a Kanban board as a simple, step-by step tracking system |
| **Strength:** Systematically keeping track of what needs to get done and checking it off her list |
| **Ways to Use Strength on the Project Team:** Create action items assigned in project team meetings, post the action items in a place that is accessible to all project team members, communicate where the action items are posted, and then create a system for marking each action item complete |

Let us add her Harmony® theme now. She could also use her Harmony® talents to help her use her Achiever® and Discipline® strength ("systematically keeping track of what needs to get done and checking it off her list") in way that is collaborative and builds relationships with her other project team members. Therefore, three of her dominant talent themes could effectively influence each other for her to develop a specific strength and use the strength in a way that benefits the project team.

| |
|---|
| **Talent Themes:** Achiever®, Discipline®, and Harmony® |
| **Specific Talent:** Drive to get things done efficiently in a collaborative way |
| **Investment:** Demonstrate the benefits and value to find agreement among the project team to consistently use a Kanban board as a simple, step-by step tracking system |
| **Strength:** Equipping the project team to collaboratively and systematically keep track of what needs to get done and checking it off the project team's list |
| **Ways to Use Strength on the Project Team:** Collaboratively create action items assigned in project team meetings, post the action items in a place that is accessible to all project team members, communicate where the action items are posted, and then create a system for marking each action item complete |

Think of some examples of how your specific talents from your top five dominant talent themes influence each other. Then think about *one of your specific strengths* which you have developed from *more than one of your dominant talent themes* that you use or could use as a project team member, project manager, or sponsor:

- What are the specific talents that you invested in?
- Which of your top five dominant talent themes are these specific talents rooted in?
- What project management tools or techniques did you invest in these specific talents?
- How could you further develop and use your project management strength?
- In what ways could you use your project management strength?

Consider adding your reflections to your talents and strengths grid and/or strengths building blocks lists.

## Summary

Project team members who are introduced to strengths development often say, "I know my top five talent themes, but I can't seem to relate them to project management." Now you have a project management connection map to help you. Having a clear understanding of your talent themes and how they are linked to project management will help you as a project manager, team member, stakeholder, or project sponsor. Maximize the connections you make between your themes and project management by also understanding how each of dominant talent themes work together. Theme dynamics is how a person's dominant themes play together, influence each other, and/or might be conflicting. To accelerate your talents and strengths development, start making the connection today!

## Key Questions

1. As a project manager, how can you use a project management connection map (the theme summaries through the lens of project management) while working with your project team? With your project sponsor?

2. Think of a time when talents from each of your talent themes have worked together, such as to complete a task, think through a situation, or work well with others. Write down your experience, describing how your dominant themes influenced each other. Then share the experience with a colleague and ask for their feedback.

3. In Exhibit 5.1, find your top five talent themes and read the project management summary description. How do these descriptions resonate with you? What other words or phrases would you use to describe your talent theme through the lens of project management? Make a list of different words or phrases that fit for you and/or your project team.

## Notes

1. Kloppenborg (2015).
2. Liesveld, C. (2014). Location 104.
3. Liesveld, C. (2014). Location 72.

## References

Kloppenborg. © 2015. *Contemporary Project Management,* 3E. South-Western, A Part of Cengage, Inc. Reproduced by Permission. www.cengage.com/permissions

Liesveld, C. 2014. *Expanding Your Strengths.* New York, NY: Gallup Press.

# CHAPTER 6

# Process: Cultivating a Strengths-Based Project Team

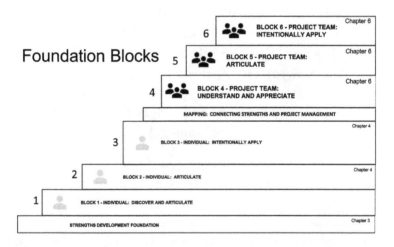

As a strengths-based project manager, your role includes creating a project team environment in which your project team members can individually and collectively engage in strengths-based talent development. You have learned about and engaged in your own individual strengths development (Chapters 3 and 4). Now your project team members also need to engage in their own individual strengths-based development, equipping them to then be able to articulate, develop, and apply their collective strengths as they work together to achieve project and team success.

In this chapter, we will be exploring how the **project team** can engage in strengths-based talent development, which are foundation blocks 4, 5 and 6 (Exhibit 6.1).

The purpose of this chapter is to help you create a strengths-based project team environment through:

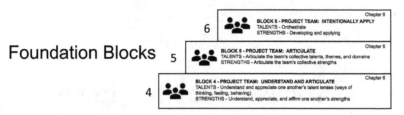

**Foundation Blocks**

Exhibit 6.1 *Project team talents and strengths development*

1. Facilitating project team member's individual strengths-based development
2. Understanding, appreciating, and articulating the collective talent themes and strengths of the project team
3. Applying the collective strengths of the project team
4. Further developing the project team's collective strengths

## Project Team Members' Individual Strengths-Based Development[1]

As a strengths-based project manager, your goal is to help your project team members *articulate* their talents and strengths and *practice* how to leverage their strengths toward the deliverables and tasks for which they are the responsible person or a key contributor.

Although individual strengths development is lifelong, the initial individual strengths development goal for your project team members is for them to have the ability to articulate their talent themes, specific talents, and strengths. This will help each team member to communicate with their project team colleagues about how they can best contribute to the project team. Project team members also need a basic understanding of how to apply their strengths to their individual tasks and goals, so that they may then learn to apply their strengths to their project team's tasks and challenges.

Take a moment to review the content and exercises presented in Chapters 3 and 4. You can use this same content to create opportunities for your project team members to begin engaging in their individual strengths-based development.

We have highlighted some of the following exercises from Chapter 4 to help you begin thinking about how best to guide your project team members in their individual strengths-based development. Although your project team members will need to do some independent reflection, your team members can also be instrumental in helping each other in their individual strengths development. Therefore, we encourage you to set aside time for your project team to learn about and engage in project team strengths conversations and exercises to equip project team members to help each other in their individual strengths development.

Invite each project team member to make a ***tabletop name card*** (instructions are in Chapter 4) and use the card as they engage in strengths-based project team conversations.

Encourage your project team members to have a ***strengths partner*** on the project team for one-to-one ongoing strengths conversations about their themes, talents, and strengths. Strengths partner conversations can be informal. As the strengths partners get to know each other and engage in strengths conversations, they will naturally figure out how they can best encourage one another. Therefore, encourage strengths partners to try to meet at least 20 minutes each week. Suggest strengths conversational prompts and ideas to your team members, which can be found in Appendix D, especially for the initial strengths partner conversations.

Project team members will also benefit from having opportunities to meet one-to-one with you (the project manager) and their functional manager. Set aside some time to meet with each of your project team members. Your initial conversational prompt with each of your project team members can simply be, "Tell me about talents from your _____ theme." (e.g., "Tell me about talents from your Input® theme.") Once your team members have more confidence in articulating their talents and strengths, then ask, "In what ways can you use your strengths on the project team?" (Look for additional strengths conversational prompts in Appendix D.)

Encourage your project team members to also have strengths conversations with their functional manager, because team members are more likely to continue strengths-based development for the long-term if their functional manager is included in their strengths-based development. Each project team member usually has a functional manager, and since each of the project team members might report to different managers, there are likely multiple functional managers connected to the project team. Each project team member should inform their functional manager that the project team is engaging in strengths development and ask their functional manager for an opportunity to have one-to-one strengths-based conversations. In Chapter 7, we will expand on the functional manager's role in supporting the project team member's individual strengths-based development.

We also suggest that you encourage each of your project team members to list their strengths building blocks (specific talents, knowledge, skills, experiences, project management tools and techniques, and specific strengths). Instructions and examples for strengths building blocks lists are in Chapter 4. Strengths building blocks lists will equip your project team members to later share with their fellow team members what they bring to the project team.

---

A word of caution… It's important for project team members to know that their privacy and talents will be respected. Before having team members share their top five talent themes with the entire project team, first introduce strengths-based development by explaining that the process is based in positive psychology. As project team members are introduced to strengths-based development, ask them for their "buy-in" and permission to share their top five with the project team.

If you have a project team member who is still not comfortable with sharing their top five themes with the team, have a one-to-one conversation with them highlighting that the themes are not to put them in a box or to label them, but to give them a starting point in which to name their unique talents and strengths. In addition, emphasize that the project team will be focusing on what is *right* with team members (positive psychology) instead of what is wrong with team members. Your positive approach to strengths-based talent development will encourage them to engage in the process.

---

## Understand, Appreciate, and Articulate the Collective Talent Themes and Strengths of the Project Team

Once each of your project team members has a good understanding of their own talent themes, unique talents, and specific strengths, they are ready to begin the *process of strengths development as a project team*.

Strengths-based project teams need opportunities for articulating the team's collective talent themes and specific strengths. The concepts and exercises presented in this chapter will help your project team members begin to understand and value each other's talents and strengths, which is an important step in working well together and a prerequisite for later intentionally leveraging the project team's collective strengths. As your project team members articulate their talents and strengths, you will develop a deeper understanding and a greater appreciation of each of your team member's specific talents within their talent themes.

Project managers are often compared to a conductor of an orchestra: It is the project manager's responsibility to lead and harmonize each instrument (person) to create melodic music (business results). Understanding your project team member's talents gives you knowledge about what motivates your team members and what your team members need to best use their strengths and work well with each other, so that you can better orchestrate the strengths of your project team.[2]

Keep in mind that each strength includes talent(s) *plus* forms of investment.

Reminder: In Chapter 3, we defined talent investment as the time and resources that you dedicate (invest) to continuously build upon your dominant talents, resulting in developing a greater strength.

A project team member's talent investment toward building a strength includes their acquired skills, knowledge, experiences, and PM tool kit.

In Chapter 2, we defined a PM tool kit as a project team member's specific project management knowledge, experiences, skills, concepts, approaches, techniques, tools, and available resources that the team member acquires and continues to add to over time. In addition, your team members will also need to acquire talent development tools to add to the *strengths development compartment* of their PM tool kit, another key element for developing their strengths.

Encourage your project team members to share their strengths with the project team. As project team members articulate and communicate their strengths to the project team, encourage them to also communicate the specific investments they made to develop their strengths, so that you and the other project team members can better understand and value what each member brings to the team.

### Understand the Principles of Strengths-Based Teams

Since you are forming a strengths-based project team and creating a strengths-based culture for your project team to further develop, you and your project team members need a basic understanding of the principles of strengths-based teams. Share what you know about strengths-based teams with your project team and consider inviting your team to read and discuss more about strengths-based teams. As you prepare to help your team learn about strengths-based team principles, consider reviewing the introduction to strengths-based teams in Chapter 3, looking over the strengths-based team resources listed in Appendix A, and reading about how to sustain a strengths-based project team culture in Chapter 7.

### Display the Top Five Talent Themes of Project Team Members

Encourage your project team members to communicate their top five talent themes to their project team members and other colleagues. They can post their top five talent themes near their desk or work station and/or in their email signature block. If you are working on a global team, consider using a "virtual white board" or other remote collaboration tools to post and share the team members' top five talent themes. Consider creating a "Project Team Talent Theme Wall," displaying each project team member's top five themes. (See sample template in Appendix B.) If your team is a virtual project team, consider how you could create a "virtual wall" where all team members could access the wall.

### Engage in Strengths Conversations

Just as in individual strengths development, strengths conversations are also important for strengths-based project team development. Here are some examples of conversational prompts that you could use to help your project team members start talking about their talents and strengths:

- Tell me about talents from two of your talent themes.
- What do you like about your talents? What is challenging about your talents?
- Did you see yourself using talents from your _____ talent theme today? In what ways?
- How have you used your talents on a project team (the current team or a previous team)?
- What project management tools or techniques have you invested in your talents? What strengths have you developed from that investment?
- More strengths conversational prompts are included in Appendix D.

Get creative with your team's strengths conversations by including strengths conversations in different contexts, such as in team meetings, at lunch or break time, and in one-to-one strengths conversations. You could also include some "fast moving" strengths conversations in your meetings. For example, for the first ten minutes of a meeting, ask your team members to talk with five other team members, asking each person a specific question (such as one of the prompts listed earlier). Allow two minutes per conversation and then move to the next person. This is an energizing way to jumpstart your project team meetings and an excellent team building exercise, which will help project team members to quickly get to know each other and work together more effectively.

### Look for Talents and Strengths in Motion

In Chapter 4, you learned about the importance of telling your colleagues and project team members when you see them using their talents and strengths. Encourage your project team members to also intentionally look for talents and strengths in motion on the project team. When team members see talents and strengths in motion, have them tell the respective project team member about the talents and strengths they saw being used. Suggest that they simply leave notes on each other's desks or on the virtual white board. Team members can also share simple verbal accolades with each other or give acknowledgement through the appropriate cultural methods of diverse, global teams.

The positivity that results from communicating talents and strengths in motion is one catalyst for starting and sustaining a strengths-based project team culture. Talents and strengths in motion is one way your project team members can support and encourage one another and may also lead to "organic" strengths conversations that start and develop naturally. This exercise also helps project team members to further their individual strengths development because their project team colleagues may bring to light new talents and strengths for them—talents and strengths they had not noticed before. Talents and strengths in motion celebrates the contributions and successes of each project team member.

### Explore the Project Team's Combined PM Tool Kit

Each team member brings their own PM tool kit with them to the project team. In individual strengths-based development, it is advantageous for project team members to understand and articulate their acquired and potential project management tools so that they can be intentional about investing these tools into their talents to develop specific *project management strengths*. Communicating and using elements of each team member's PM tool kit is also important for the project team's success. A project team's awareness of the elements from the team member's PM tool kits will increase the likelihood that the team will intentionally use elements from their combined PM tool kits and more effectively leverage their team's collective strengths toward their project (Exhibit 6.2).

Prior to the project kick-off meeting, or early-on in the project, have each project team member think about their PM tool kit and encourage each project team member to:

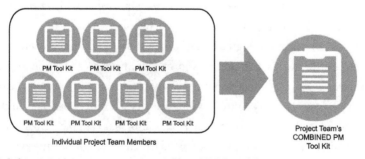

Exhibit 6.2  A project team's combined PM tool kit

- Prepare a list of key project management tools, techniques, knowledge, and experiences which they have acquired
- Keep track of their general skills, knowledge and experiences, which may not be project management specific but can also benefit the project team
- Consider forming a list of project management tools and techniques which they are interested in acquiring or acquired tools and techniques which they would like to build upon

Give your project team members the freedom in how to best articulate their own PM tool kit. Your team members may use specific project management key words to describe elements of their PM tool kit; however, your team members may also bring to the table a unique combination of tools, techniques, and/or combination of general skills, knowledge, and experiences which they integrate into managing and working on projects. Giving project team members the flexibility in *how* they articulate and describe their own PM tool kit elements will help the project team to better understand specifically what each project team member brings to the team. Furthermore, flexibility in articulating their PM tool kits will also help team members articulate their unique, specific *project management strengths*.

As your team members share the specific project management knowledge, skills, experiences, and competencies which they bring to the team, begin creating a [name of project team] ***Project Team's Combined PM Tool Kit*** (see Exhibit 6.2).

After your project team has articulated and discussed the ***Project Team's Combined PM Tool Kit***, say to the team:

Combining each of our PM tool kits, plus our other general skills, knowledge, and experiences, are important components of the strengths each of us brings to the project team! Look at our long list of tools that we can use as we intentionally apply our strengths toward our team challenges! As you acquire new tools, add your new tools to your own PM tool kit and our ***Project Team's Combined PM Tool Kit.***

Throughout the life of the project, and working together as a project team, encourage your team to continue adding to your **Project Team's Combined PM Tool Kit**. As the team continues to add to the list, encourage team members to be creative, giving team members the freedom to best articulate and add their project management tools and techniques, and other tools they acquire and bring to the project team. You will use this list again later when your project team intentionally applies the team's strengths toward the team's challenges.

Decide where your project team will keep your **Project Team's Combined PM Tool Kit** so that it is accessible for project team meetings and available to each of your project team members. When you are working on a global project team, use remote collaboration tools to make the list available to all of the project team members.

### List the Project Team's Current Strengths

When your team is engaging in strengths-based project team development, using the basic and common language of the CliftonStrengths Themes will help simplify the process. However, it is essential that your team members also be intentional about articulating their individual strengths, which will help the project team to better understand and maximize their collective strengths.

Give your team members opportunities to share with each other the strengths they bring to the project team and what they need from other project team members to maximize the use of their strengths on the team. Ask your project team members:

- What strengths do you bring to the team?
- What do you need to maximize the strengths you bring to the project team?
- What strengths do you need from the team?

Encourage your team members to be creative in articulating the strengths they bring to the project team. Your project team members will name their specific project management strengths, but they may

*Exhibit 6.3  The ABC project team's collective strengths list*

| Team member | Specific strengths—consistent, proficient ability to: |
|---|---|
| Joe | Present complex project management topics to large groups |
| Susie | Connect people with people through email and social media to increase stakeholder engagement |
| Charles | Arrange details quickly staying attuned to the timing of the event and/or tasks |
| Allen | Interpret statistical data for others based on the individual's ability to understand statistical data |
| Sabrina | Mentor individuals toward their growth and development |
| Sally | Create compelling visuals (charts, diagrams) to quickly demonstrate project management concepts, tools, techniques |

also name strengths that do not seem to be related to project management. Pay attention! Strengths used in other areas of life (at home, in the community, volunteering, at school, at work, etc.) may also be helpful as the team addresses their project team challenges. Therefore, keep track of the project team's non-specific project management strengths too.

As project team members share their specific strengths, begin listing their strengths in a [name of project team] **Project Team's Collective Strengths List** (Exhibit 6.3), which will give the team a visual list for a deeper awareness of the team's collective strengths.

You will use your team's **Project Team's Collective Strengths List** when your project team intentionally applies the team's strengths toward the team's challenges.

After the team has had the time to list their specific, collective strengths, encourage your project team members to refer to your **Project Team Member's Combined PM Tool Kit** as the team responds to the following prompts:

- What project team successes have resulted from team member(s) using specific elements from their PM tool kit?
- What specific strengths have resulted from team members investing elements from their PM tool kit into their talents?

(You may want to use talent theme language here for a simpler talent language.)

- Which of the team's specific project management strengths has helped the project team be successful?
- Which of the team's non-specific project management strengths has helped the project team be successful? (Non-specific project management strengths are strengths not necessarily developed by project management specific knowledge/skills/experience).
- How could the team use their specific strength(s) in the future?

As your project team discusses the preceding questions, your team will probably name additional project management tools they have acquired and more current strengths to add to your team's *Project Team's Combined PM Tool Kit* and *Project Team's Collective Strengths List*. Furthermore, throughout the life of your project team, encourage your team members to continue adding to your *Project Team's Combined PM Tool Kit* and *Project Team's Collective Strengths List*.

Decide where your project team will keep your team's *Project Team's Collective Strengths List* so that it is accessible for project team meetings and available to each of your project team members—both onsite and remote.

### Other Resources for Articulating Team Talents, Investments, and Strengths

We have listed just a few strengths-based practices and exercises to help your project team members get started articulating their collective talents and strengths, which will prepare your project team to be intentional about applying their strengths toward your project. We encourage you to consider other resources available to you, which will give you more practices and exercises for helping your project team dive deeper into articulating their talents and strengths. Some of these resources are listed in Appendix A.

## Applying the Collective Strengths of the Project Team

> Strengths-based project teams integrate their knowledge, skills, and practice of strengths development with project management tools and techniques, equipping the project team to **apply** and maximize their collective strengths to successfully complete their project on time, within budget, and according to the project objectives and specifications.

Once project team members are engaged in individual strengths-based talent development, have developed an understanding and appreciation of each other's talents, and have articulated the team's strengths, they are then ready to *apply* their strengths to the project—as individuals and as a project team. For example, each strengths-based project team member is equipped to intentionally apply their strengths toward deliverables or tasks for which they are responsible or contributing effort. In addition, the project team has the ability to work together in applying their collective strengths toward their *specific project team challenges*.

Every project team has challenges: some challenges are common project team challenges, and some are unique. Take time as a project team to think about and identify your *specific* project team challenges, such as dealing with a difficult situation or problem.

- What external factors are influencing or impacting the project?
- What internal factors (like ongoing work) are having an impact on the project?
- What is the culture of trust and discipline among the project team?
- How can you utilize the collective talents, skills, knowledge, experiences, and strengths of the project team to help identify the challenge?

Although there are many approaches toward applying the collective strengths of a project team, here is one four-step application approach:

Step 1: Gather your project team's talent themes, PM tool kit, and strengths

Step 2: Choose a specific task or team challenge

Step 3: Indicate the best project management tools, techniques, and strengths to use to address the challenge

Step 4: Create an action plan for applying the project team's collective strengths

You have already been introduced to the **prework** required to prepare your project team to engage in this four-step application approach (Chapters 3, 4, and the beginning of this chapter). Before engaging in the four-step approach, your project team members first need to:

- Be engaged in individual strengths development, having the ability to:
  - Describe specific talents from each of their top five talent themes
  - Articulate some of their specific strengths
  - Intentionally invest in their talents toward strengths
- Have practiced articulating the collective talent themes and strengths of their project team
- Be engaged in a basic level of strengths-based project team development
- Have listed the project team's collective talent themes, project management tools, and strengths, such as the lists you made previously:
  - Project team's combined PM tool kit (shown previously)
  - Project team's collective strengths list (shown previously)
- Discussed and documented their team challenges

### Step One: Gather Your Project Team's Talent Themes, PM Tool Kit, and Strengths

- Project team's collective talent themes
  - Make your project team's talent themes available and visible:
    - Invite each project team member to use their *tabletop name card* so that the other team members can see their top five talent themes.

- Give each project team member a copy of your *project team's collective talent themes* (each member's name with their respective talent themes).
  - You can also organize your project team's talents themes by the CliftonStrengths Domains. A team talent theme grid organized by the CliftonStrengths Domains can give the project team a good visual and simple format for exploring the project team's collective talents and potential strength. See Appendix A for Gallup resources to use to learn more about and how to use the CliftonStrengths Domains.
- Project team's combined PM tool kit
- Project team's collective strengths list

### Step Two: Choose a Specific Project Team Challenge

Which of your current team challenges would you like to focus on now? As a project team, describe the team challenge in detail.

### Step Three: Indicate the Best Project Management Tools, Techniques, and Strengths to Use

As the project team considers their collective project management tools, techniques, and strengths that the team could *potentially* use to approach its team challenge, lead your project team discussion with the following prompts:

- How has the team leveraged their strengths toward a similar challenge in the past?
- What strengths do team members have that could help address this team challenge successfully?
- In what specific ways could team members contribute to addressing this challenge?
- What potential complementary partnerships could the project team members form to address this challenge?

### Step Four: Create an Action Plan for Applying the Project Team's Collective Strengths

After your project team has discussed potential ways to approach your project team challenge, then your project team is equipped to decide and articulate how the team members will apply their strengths and their PM tool kits toward your team's challenge—this is your action plan. Once again, be creative as you articulate your action plan to best fit your project team's needs and style.

Applying your project team's strengths takes practice! After you create and implement your action plan, then repeat steps one through four again, working to leverage your project team's collective strengths toward another one of your team's challenges.

As your project team continues to practice this four-step application process, your team may organically develop other strengths application processes that work best for your project team. In addition, as your project team practices applying their strengths, your team will begin to naturally weave strengths conversations into your planning meetings and decision processes, and you will naturally leverage and maximize your project team's strengths.

Be sure to keep track of the challenges your team successfully overcomes from applying your project team's collective strengths toward those challenges. (See template in Appendix B). Reflecting on these successes will motivate your project team members to continue developing and applying their strengths.

## Continuous Strengths Development for Project Teams

Strengths-based project teams are intentional about continuously developing their project team's collective strengths. One of the techniques used in project management is documenting lessons learned on projects. The purpose of lessons learned is to make continuous improvements as you work on similar projects in the future. The same is true in continuous improvement of yourself and your project team through ongoing development of your collective strengths. This doesn't happen overnight. It takes time, patience, focus, and an action plan.

There are specific approaches for continuous strengths development for your project team, which are beyond the scope of this book. See Appendix A for resources to continue your project team's strengths development.

## Summary

Many of the strengths development steps and principles that you and your project team members can use for *individual* strengths development can also be applied to *group* strengths development—your project team. Set aside time for your project team members to learn about and engage in team strengths conversations and exercises to support project team members' individual strengths development. Look for, recognize, and acknowledge when you see talents and strengths in motion for starting and sustaining a strengths-based project team culture. Engage in continuous strengths development for your project team members and project team. Strengths-based project teams combine and use their PM tool kits, along with their collective strengths, to be a high performing strengths-based project team. Applying your project team's strengths takes practice—it's not too late to start practicing!

## Key Questions

1. From your perspective, what does a strengths-based project team look like?
2. If you had facilitated project team strengths development on a previous project, how do you think it would have impacted or improved the working relationship of the team members? How would it have impacted or improved the project team's results?
3. Think about facilitating strengths-based development for your current and/or next project team:
   (a) What successes and/or challenges do you envision if you were to guide your project team in the process of becoming a strengths-based project team?
   (b) What actions or exercises would you put in place for getting started? Make a list of five to ten items.

# Notes

1. Some project managers enjoy leading and facilitating the initial strengths development processes for their project teams. However, some project managers prefer having some assistance in the initial stages of becoming a strengths-based project team. You have available to you Gallup-Certified Strengths Coaches who can work with you and your project team. In addition, Gallup sells team tool kits, which will give you more ideas and exercises for working with your team. (See Appendix A.)
2. Hafzoglu and Öztürk (2009).

# Reference

Hafzoglu, M., and M.C. Öztürk. 2009. "What Does a Conductor of an Orchestra Actually Do?" Paper Presented At PMI® Global Congress 2009—EMEA, Amsterdam, North Holland, The Netherlands. Newtown Square, PA: Project Management Institute.

# CHAPTER 7

# Sustaining: Keeping a Strengths-Based Project Team Culture Going

PROJECT SPONSOR
Your Champion

SUSTAINING A STRENGTHS - BASED PROJECT TEAM CULTURE

FUNCTIONAL MANAGERS
Your Advocates

The collective involvement of these roles is the essential glue in keeping a strengths-based project team culture going.

PROJECT TEAM MEMBERS
Your Gears

PROJECT MANAGER
Your Conductor

The initial process of becoming a strengths-based project team is often new, exciting, and has momentum. Furthermore, the process takes time, energy, and resources. Working together as a team, you want your project team to continue to be a strengths-based project team over the life of the project—and beyond. This sustained effort enables you to truly maximize the investment you have made. How can you receive a long-term return on your initial strengths development investment and sustain your project team's strengths-based momentum?

Further cultivating your ***project team's strengths-based culture*** will yield a high return and continue to energize your team. In the process of developing your strengths-based project team, you have already started to develop a strengths-based culture. Your strengths-based culture flows from your project team members' engagement and attitude toward the project team developing and using their strengths. A long-term strengths-based culture includes fertile ground for ongoing support, encouragement, and opportunities for project team members to develop and use their strengths every day.

The purpose of this chapter is to help you to see the importance of sustaining a strengths-based project team culture and how the following project management roles impact the culture:

1. The role of the project sponsor
2. The role of the functional managers
3. The role of the project manager
4. The role of all the project team members

Each of these project management roles is essential in creating and sustaining the strengths-based project team culture. Although the ways in which each of the different project management roles can influence and effect a strengths-based culture are distinct, they also have some commonalities and are closely interrelated. The collective involvement of these roles in the project team's strengths-based development is the essential glue in keeping a strengths-based project team culture going.

One added note: How your organization is structured (projectized, matrix, functional, multi-divisional, etc.) may have a direct impact and influence on how you could best introduce, develop, and sustain a strengths-based project team culture. As you begin working with this process, think about how the process will work best and be accepted/supported in your company culture and structure.

## The Role of the Project Sponsor

PROJECT SPONSOR
Your Champion

The project sponsor is the project team's ***champion*** for sustaining their strengths-based project team culture. In Chapter 2, we defined a project sponsor as a person, a group of people, or an organization who has authorized the project team to do the project. By definition, the project sponsor has ultimate control over the project, in that it is the project sponsor who is providing the resources, funding, permission, and support to do the project. Project sponsors influence the successful sustainability of a long-term strengths-based project team culture for their project teams when the project sponsor leads by example, provides support, and celebrates strengths-based project team successes.

Strengths-based project sponsors lead by example when they positively engage in their own strengths-development and then leverage their strengths in their sponsor role. As project team members see their sponsor engaging in the sponsor's own strengths development and application, team members begin to trust that a long-term strengths-based project team culture will be sustained. This can motivate team members to more fully engage in developing and applying *their* strengths.

The project sponsor has some influence in providing what the project team needs to be a successful project team. Therefore, the sponsor may have some influence in providing resources and funding for initial and long-term strengths-based project team development. The sponsor can positively influence the project team's strengths development success when the sponsor keeps the communication channels open with the project team to learn what the team needs for their continued strengths-based development, growth, and application.

Finally, the sponsor influences the sustainability of the project team's strengths-based culture when the sponsor takes the time to celebrate the project team's strengths-based successes with the team. Just like in the other project roles, project sponsors should be looking for and acknowledging *talents and strengths in motion* from the project team members. When they see project team members using their talents and strengths and tell the team members what they see, their positive comments further cultivate the sustainability of the project team's strengths-based culture.

## The Role of the Functional Managers

The functional managers of the project team members contribute to influencing and impacting a strengths-based project team culture. Project team members' functional managers are their short and long-term strengths development ***advocates***, during the project and after the project's completion. When each project team member starts individual strengths

FUNCTIONAL MANAGERS
Your Advocates

development with their functional manager's positive and knowledgeable support, each team member is likely to fully engage in and continue developing and applying their strengths, maximizing the organization's project team strengths-development return on investment.

Functional managers are in a position to provide their direct reports consistent, long-term mentoring and development. The functional manager has the ongoing responsibility and capability to influence their direct report's receptiveness toward and opportunities for developing their strengths—as an individual contributor and a project team member. If project team members' functional managers believe and engage in strengths development, then project team members have greater trust that the organization's support of developing and using their strengths will be sustained. Trust in strengths sustainability will motivate project team members to more deeply engage in their project team's strengths development process.

Once project team members begin the process of developing and using their strengths, they will want to continue the process even after the project is completed. Most often, project sponsors and project managers directly work with their project team members only for the length of the project. When the project ends, each team member may go to another project team—with a different project manager and perhaps a different project sponsor—or maybe back to their regular job working full-time for their functional manager. Therefore, the functional manager's support is critical for each project team member's long-term strengths engagement and career development. The functional manager can continue to provide their direct reports with what they need to continue developing and using their strengths—doing what they do best at work every day.

Even when a strengths-based project team disbands, project team members have the potential to bring their previous project team's strengths-based culture into other project teams. Functional managers' initial and long-term support will also increase the likelihood that project team members will use their strengths on future project teams, possibly influencing and leading to a strengths-based project team organizational norm.

Who has the responsibility to inform each project team member's functional manager about the team becoming a strengths-based project team? Each project team member!

There is a twofold advantage for each of the project team members to be the person who informs their own functional manager about the team's strengths-based development. First, since each team member usually has a functional manager, there can be as many functional managers as there are team members. Take a project team of five people: the team can have as many as five functional managers. Therefore, it could be a time-consuming task for the project manager to communicate in depth with each functional manager about the project team's strengths-based development engagement and the talents and strengths of the functional manager's respective direct report.

The second advantage, and more importantly, is that the project team member is taking an active role in being responsible for their own individual strengths development. The one-to-one communication between the functional manager and the project team member will allow time for the team member to articulate their talents and strengths and explain the strengths development process that the project team is engaging in. The functional manager will then have opportunity to ask questions and engage in strengths conversations with their direct report.

Although project team members have the ultimate responsibility to inform their functional manager about strengths development on the project team, project sponsors and project managers need to support and equip team members to inform and engage in strengths conversations with their functional managers. Equipping project team members to have strengths conversations can include giving them a list of ideas for starting the conversations, such as:

- Sharing their themes, talents, and strengths
- Explaining how they are developing their strengths
- Showing how they want to continue developing and using their strengths
- Sharing how they want to leverage their strengths in situations which seem to require their lesser talents
- Exploring strengths resources that would help the functional manager understand strengths development and application

## The Role of the Project Manager

PROJECT MANAGER
Your Conductor

The project manager is the **conductor** of the strengths-based project team: the project manager is leading and directing the team's strengths development and application opportunities. A project manager can successfully contribute to sustaining the project team's strengths-based culture by developing and using their own strengths as they lead, manage, support, and encourage their project team members to do the same. As a project manager engages in the process of investing in developing and using their strengths, they become a better project manager—*and the project team notices!*

When project managers develop and use their own strengths, they are "modeling" what it means to be a strengths-based project team member. For example, when the project manager includes her top five dominant themes in her email signature block and posts her top five themes on her desk, she is modeling strengths-based practices for her project team members.

Strengths-based project managers also help sustain the strengths-based culture by positively leading, encouraging, and equipping their team members to engage in and be responsible for their own long-term strengths development. For the duration of the project, project managers need to provide opportunities for the team to continue to learn about strengths philosophy and apply what they learn on the project team.

A sustained strengths-based culture includes the project manager encouraging team members to use their strengths toward the project. Strengths-based project managers value each team member and what each team member brings to the project team. They encourage team members to use their strengths to best contribute to the project team. They create an atmosphere for project team members to share with the team their talents and strengths so that they can articulate how they can best contribute to the team and ways to use their strengths in their roles rather than using their lesser talents.

Therefore, the project manager is setting the stage for their team members to also encourage each other. Team members need to take notice when their colleagues use their strengths and then share what they see with their fellow team members. Strengths-based project managers lead their project team to understand that their talent and strength differences are an advantage for the team and that they need each other to get the project accomplished. They encourage their team to form strengths-based complementary partnerships as they approach tasks and challenges.

A strengths-based project team culture depends on strengths conversations. Therefore, project managers need to weave strengths conversations into their project team meetings and when they meet one-to-one with their team members. They also need to encourage their team members to have strengths conversations outside of team meetings. Project managers model effective strengths conversations by asking good questions and listening carefully as their team members share their talents and strengths with them and the project team.

Once again, sustaining a strengths-based project team culture requires the involvement of all of the project team members' functional managers. Strengths-based project managers encourage and equip their project team members to reach out to their functional manager about their individual and project team strengths-based development. Project managers can supply their team members with strengths-based resources and conversational prompts to help them share their themes, talents, and strengths with their functional manager. This is one way to equip team members to take charge of their own individual strengths development for sustaining the long-term use and development of their strengths. (See Appendix D for more conversational prompt ideas.)

As the project manager uses their own strengths and encourages others to do the same, the project team members begin to trust that the team will function long-term as a strengths-based project team, creating a culture where team members can use their strengths on the team. The project manager is continually seeking and identifying opportunities for utilizing a team member's individual strengths on the project. This creates synergies for a greater project impact. It is essential that the project manager gives genuine praise and credit by linking an individual's strengths to the project impact.

## The Role of All Project Team Members

PROJECT TEAM MEMBERS
Your Gears

Project team members are the *gears* that keep the strengths-based project team culture going for their team. Each team member needs to engage in the **full strengths development model** of discovering, appreciating, articulating, and applying their talents and strengths—applying this model again and again.

It is "nice" to know about our talents and see how we are using them in our lives now; however, sustaining a strengths-based project team culture requires team members to continually, intentionally apply their strengths: First, investing in talents toward strengths and further developing strengths; then, intentionally leveraging existing strengths toward deliverables, tasks, and team challenges. As project team members continue to practice developing and applying their own strengths, they also need to encourage each other in the process.

As assignments or responsibilities are accepted by team members for deliverables and tasks, a strengths-based culture is further developed when project team members intentionally factor-in team members' specific strengths in the assignment process by asking themselves:

- How can we maximize our collective strengths toward this deliverable? Toward this task?
- What team member(s) have the strengths to best carryout this task?

And once tasks are assigned, strengths-based project team members need to reflect on how they can best use their strengths to accomplish their respective tasks.

The process of how the team can best apply their strengths is also important for project team challenges. What are the team's challenges? How can the project team's collective strengths be used to best approach a specific challenge? Periodically revisiting the team's challenges will help maximize the application of the team's collective strengths, further strengthening the team's strengths-based culture.

Project team members also effect a strengths-based culture when they take ownership of their own ongoing strengths development. Once again, each project team member needs to take the responsibility for informing their functional manager about their strengths development—what the team member is doing about and with strengths development—and seeking their functional manager's support for keeping it going. In addition, each project team member needs to engage in ongoing one-to-one strengths conversations with their functional manager, project manager, and strengths partner (Chapters 4 and 6) for uncovering untapped talent and further developing their strengths.

Awareness of a team member's individual strengths and their impact on project work is fundamental. However, awareness of the individual strengths of the other team members is equally important. Identifying ways to combine and collaborate the team's collective strengths to create project impact will help sustain a strengths-based culture.

Finally, it is critical that each team member is contributing their insights, ideas, and strengths while working together as a strengths-based project team to sustain a strengths-based culture.

## Summary

In order to sustain a strengths-based project team culture, and further develop that culture, the project sponsor, functional managers, the project manager, and all project team members need to be on board. It is the collective involvement of these roles that provides the essential glue in keeping a strengths-based project team culture going.

Project sponsors can influence the successful sustainability of a long-term strengths-based project team culture when they lead by example, provide support, and celebrate strengths-based project team success. The functional manager of each project team member can influence and impact the sustainability of a strengths-based culture by providing their direct reports with consistent, long-term mentoring and development. The project manager needs to seek opportunities for the team to continue to learn about strengths philosophy and apply what they learn on the project team. And all of the project team members need to take ownership to engage and apply their own ongoing strengths development.

The whole project team is in this together—everyone is the glue to sustaining a strengths-based project team culture.

## Key Questions

1. When you think of "owning" your own strengths development, what does that mean to you? What steps would you put in place to demonstrate your ownership to your functional manager, project manager, project sponsor, or team colleagues?

2. Think about the strengths-based project team culture in your current project, department, or organization. What does it look like today? What could it look like in the future? How can you contribute to establishing, growing, and sustaining a strengths-based project team culture?

3. Imagine a one-to-one conversation with your functional manager about your interest in strengths development. What would be the top three things that you would share with your functional manager? What support would you need from your functional manager to continue your strengths development?

# CHAPTER 8

# Action Plan: Make an Investment

Just like a project plan, you need a **focused action plan** for investing in talent development for yourself and your project team. Nothing gets done unless you take action! And a plan helps you to identify where you are going and what it takes to get there.

We will continue using the strengths-based talent development model that we have been using throughout the book for explaining how to develop and implement a focused action plan for investing in talent development. This section is designed for you (as an individual) and for your project team (as a group).

The purpose of this chapter is to help you:

1. Prepare to take action
2. Take action—breaking strengths-based project team development into manageable pieces
3. Develop a focused action plan
4. Bring it all together!

## Prepare to Take Action

Before preparing a talent development focused action plan, have a good personal understanding of why you are choosing to move forward with talent development for you and your project team:

- Why specifically do you want to invest talent development?
- What are you trying to accomplish?
- What is your vision?

Your responses to the preceding questions may include that as a project manager, you are focused on working with your project team and key stakeholders to deliver the project objective. When you add the element of talent development into your focus, it increases your project team's potential to deliver your project on time, within budget, according to the project objective and specifications. We encourage you to be even more specific: articulate specific ways that you think talent development will help your unique project team to be a high-performing project team.

Once you have a good foundation in understanding why you want to invest in talent development, then you need to choose a talent development model.

- What type of talent development do you want to implement?
- What talent development models are available to you and your team?
- What type of talent development model does your company already use?
- What would your company's response be to you introducing a new form of talent development to your project team?
- How much time do you want to invest in talent development? Do you want your team members to have a basic awareness of talent development or develop and use their talents for the long-term?

If your talent development approach includes strengths-based development, your talent development vision will include developing a high-performance project team by ongoing development and application of the project team's collective strengths. Your project team's **Strengths-Based Talent Development Action Plan** will include the specifics of "how" you will implement your vision:

- How specifically will you build and sustain your high performing strengths-based project team?
- How will you add talent development to your PM tool kit?

- What exercises will you choose to best help your project team to become a strengths-based project team?
- What will you do to sustain a strengths-based project team culture?

Just like you have invested in project management development, it is now time to invest in talent and strengths development.

## Take Action—Breaking It Down

In project management, the work breakdown structure (WBS) tool is instrumental in helping the project team break down the work into manageable pieces. We encourage you to use this same approach as you break down the processes you will use for engaging in talent development. To break down your own strengths-based talent development goals and your project team's goals into manageable pieces, consider these timeframes:

- Short-term goals: action items that you commit to getting done within the next six months
- Mid-term goals: action items that you commit to getting done in six months to one year
- Long-term goals: action items that you commit to getting done that will take longer than one year

Notice that each type of time-specific goal description includes the word "commit." Taking action includes taking **ownership** and holding yourself accountable for your progress and results. Strengths development for yourself and your project team takes commitment, dedication, and self-discipline for maximum return on your investment.

## Professional Development Plan

Where do you start? We suggest that you start by putting your strength development action items into a professional development plan. What is a professional development plan?

> The personal or **professional development plan** (PDP) is a formal means by which an individual (normally working with a teacher, mentor, or supervisor) sets out the goals, strategies, and outcomes of learning and training.[1]

A PDP is a guide for your career development. Once you design and create your specific, unique PDP, your PDP can serve as a roadmap to lead and support your commitment for continuous improvement. If you already have a PDP, great! Add your focused action plan items for strengths development to your existing PDP. If you do not have a PDP, or need a PDP template, see Exhibit 8.1. Feel free to modify the template to fit your needs.

In addition to the PDP template's time-specific goal descriptions (left-hand column), you will notice that there are suggested specific developmental categories (across the top) to provide focus.

The PDP categories indicated in Exhibit 8.1 and as described in Exhibit 8.2 are especially helpful for individuals and project teams engaging in strengths-based development: the organizational knowledge, functional skills, and project management categories are project management specific developmental categories, which are also talent investment

**Exhibit 8.1** *Professional development plan template*

| Category | Organizational Knowledge | Functional Skills | Project Management | Strengths Development |
|---|---|---|---|---|
| Short-term goals (1 to 6 months) | | | | |
| Mid-term goals (6 months to 1 year) | | | | |
| Long-term goals (greater than 1 year) | | | | |

*Exhibit 8.2  Professional development plan category explanation*

| Category | Purpose | Comment |
|---|---|---|
| Organizational knowledge | Learn more about the company or department | What activities could you do to improve your knowledge about the company, its products or services, or its customers? |
| Functional skills | Learn more about what you do "every day" | What activities could you do to improve your ability to do your day-to-day work or take your abilities to the next level? |
| Project management | Learn more about managing projects and people (team members) | If you are a project manager, what activities could you do to improve your ability to create a strengths-based project team? |
| Strengths development | Learn more about your individual talents and strengths | For strengths development, what activities could you put in place to discover, appreciate, articulate, and intentionally apply your talents and strengths? |

ingredients for strengths development. Using your adaptability skills, pick the categories or add more categories that best fit your developmental needs.

While the PDP is primarily designed for individual development, you could modify the PDP framework for your project team's development.

## Suggestions for a Focused Action Plan

In each chapter, there are references to action planning. Consider the book's action planning ideas to assist you in developing your **focused action plan**. To help you get started with your own focused action plan, we have provided a comprehensive list of the book's key action planning suggestions with brief summaries describing the actions. Each summary also includes a chapter reference so that you can refer back to the chapter for more action planning details.

Having a focused action plan means to prioritize. Consider taking the following items and populating them in your PDP template—with short-term, mid-term, and long-term goals. Do not try to take on all of these suggestions at once. Create a reasonable plan that works for you and is achievable for you!

Again, many of the following suggestions can work for both you as an individual and for your project team as a group.

### Keep Growing Your Strengths List (Chapter 1)

At the start of this book, you listed three things that you consistently do well. Keep this list going. It is an excellent tool to showcase your strengths.

### Conduct a Shared Expectations Exercise (Chapter 2)

Look for opportunities where you and a team can create a shared expectations document. This could be any team—a project team, work team, mentor team, community team, manager/employee team, and so on. See the instructions in Chapter 2. Give it a try!

### Take the CliftonStrengths (StrengthsFinder) Assessment (Chapter 4)

This is where strengths development begins. See Chapter 4 for details. Once you have taken the assessment tool and have obtained your top five talent themes, memorize them. Share them with others. Read more about each of your talent themes in the various reports, and/or in the Clifton-Strengths books. See Appendix A for additional resources.

### Use Your CliftonStrengths Reports (Chapter 4)

1. Signature Themes Report
2. Strengths Insight Report
3. Strengths Insight and Action-Planning Guide

### Print a Copy of Your Reports

Read over your top five talent theme summaries in your *Signature Themes Report* and highlight words and phrases in your top five theme summaries that describe you. Begin articulating some of your specific talents from the words and phrases that you highlighted.

Review the three key sections of your *Strengths Insight and Action-Planning Guide*: awareness, application, and achievement.

After your review and reflection, add the action steps you are planning to take to your PDP. Add your CliftonStrengths reports to your PM tool kit. See Chapter 4 for detailed instructions.

### Create a Tabletop Name Card (Chapters 4 and 6)

Your tabletop name card has two sides: a front and a back. Write your first name and your top five talent themes on both sides. Place your tabletop name card on your desk, carry it with you to meetings, and use it as you engage in one-to-one strengths conversations.

### Develop Your Strengths Building Blocks Lists (Chapter 4)

Your strengths building blocks lists includes your specific talents, skills, knowledge, experiences, and specific strengths. Continue to grow your "working document." (Exhibit 8.3)

### Practice a Talent Theme a Day (Chapter 4)

Choose one of your top five dominant talent themes. On the first day, notice how you naturally use that talent. Write down specific talents within this theme that you used during the day. Over the next few days, find two ways to intentionally leverage the specific talent. Continue this process by adding to your strengths building blocks lists. Repeat the process for the other four talent themes.

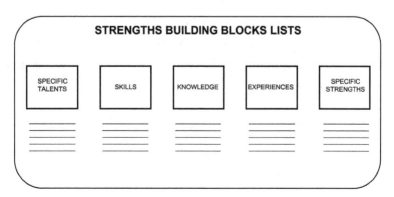

*Exhibit 8.3 Working document for your strengths building blocks lists*

### Hold-Up the Mirror (Chapter 4)

Describe your top five talent themes to a team member, project manager, project sponsor, colleague, or someone outside the project. Engage others in strengths conversations.

### Build a Strengths Partnership (Chapter 4)

Find someone who is also interested in strengths development. Meet with your strengths partner once or twice a week for 20 minutes for strengths conversations. Encourage your team members to develop strengths partnerships as well.

### Use "My Talents and Strengths Grid" (Chapter 4)

Use your grid to keep track of your ideas for developing your talent potential and ways that you have already successfully invested in your specific talents.

### Look for Talents and Strengths in Motion (Chapters 4 and 6)

When you see one of your colleagues or project team members using their talents and strengths, tell them! It can be a simple note that you leave on their desk or a simple verbal accolade. If you are working on a global project team, consider the different country cultures for sharing this information.

### Meet with Your Functional Manager (Chapters 6 and 7)

Have a strengths development conversation with your boss. Keep your functional manager informed of your progress. Share your PDP—professional development plan. Review your PDP together for support and mutual understanding.

### Create a "Project Team Talent Theme Wall" (Chapter 6)

Showcase the collective talent themes of the project team on a wall or virtual white board. Display everyone's top five talent themes in some way.

### List the Project Team's Collective Strengths (Chapter 6)

Use the strengths building blocks lists to capture all of the strengths of the project team.

### Use a PM Connection Map (Chapter 5)

Find, read about, and reflect on your top five talent themes in the "Strengths Themes as Used in Project Management" chart (Exhibit 5.1 and Appendix C). Have your project team members do the same. Have a strengths-based conversation with your project team by inviting team members to share their reflections with each other.

As mentioned in the beginning of this book, use your creativity and adaptability skills to modify your PDP and focused action plan in a way that fits for you. The aforementioned suggestions are simply to get you started. Add other ideas to your PDP that are unique to you and your team's development needs.

## Summary

### Let's Bring It All Together!

Vincent Van Gogh, the Dutch Post-Impressionist painter and writer, once said: "Great things are not done by impulse, but by a series of small things brought together."

This book is the start of small things brought together—to help you discover and develop the talents and strengths within you—and the talents and strengths within your project team.

We encourage you to use this book as you engage in a lifetime investment of strengths development. Strengths-based project team development is an ongoing, continuous developmental cycle, requiring investment of time and energy. As you and your project team begin engaging in strengths-based talent development, experiment, try things out, make adjustments, practice, and have strengths-based conversations with your team members. Explore your talents and expand your confidence in developing and using your own strengths. Build on the strengths that you already have, while you develop new strengths. Apply the book's tools and techniques to your unique project team. Use your PDP as a guide, referencing it frequently, celebrating your successes, making necessary adjustments and modifications, and adding new items as you continue to practice and grow personally and professionally.

Working together, you and your project team members can each do small things *every day* to become a strengths-based project team, sustain your strengths-based project team culture, and leverage your strengths toward your project. It is through your continuous commitment, efforts, focus, and working with your PDP that you will be successful in reaching your goals. And as you travel the strengths-based project team journey, who knows what new doors of opportunity might open for you, for those around you, and for your project team.

Take time to reflect, learn, and grow.

## Key Questions

1. Draft your detailed focused action plan and share it with your boss or trusted colleague. Ask for their help with accountability. What is needed for you to achieve each milestone listed in the focused action plan?
2. Pick one or two items in the focused action planning suggestions, shown earlier. What is your commitment to achieve these items? How will you achieve them?
3. Create and follow a PDP. Use it as a roadmap to grow your own strengths and the strengths of your project team.

## Note

1. Definition of Professional Development Plan (2018).

## Reference

"Definition of Professional Development Plan." 2018. http://faculty.london deanery.ac.uk/e-learning/assessing-educational-needs-1/personal-or-professional-development-plans (accessed March 23, 2018).

# APPENDIX A

# Resources

## Project Management Resources

### Books Published by BEP

Project Management Essentials, by Kathryn Wells and Timothy Kloppenborg, 2016.

Project Teams: A Structured Development Approach, by Vittal Anantatmula, 2016.

### Books and Reports Published by the Project Management Institute

PMBOK® Guide. A Guide to the Project Management Body of Knowledge (Sixth Edition). 2017. https://pmi.org/pmbok-guide-standards/foundational/pmbok/sixth-edition

PM Curriculum and Resources. Volume III: Project Teams, Leadership and Communication PM-2. 2017. https://pmiteach.org/teaching-pm/

PMI Pulse of the Profession reports. https://pmi.org/learning/thought-leadership/pulse

Project Manager Competency Development Framework. Third Edition. 2017. https://pmi.org/pmbok-guide-standards/framework/pm-competency-development-3rd-edition

## Strengths-Based Talent Development Resources

### Gallup Strengths Center (www.gallupstrengthscenter.com)

Many resources are available to you at the Gallup Strengths Center website. When you took the CliftonStrengths (StrengthsFinder) assessment, you set up an online CliftonStrengths account at the Gallup Strengths Center website. Login again, take a look around, and note the resources that are available to you at the website.

## Books Published by Gallup, Inc.

Gallup, Inc. has many strengths-based talent development books. Listed as follows are several books that may be helpful for project teams that are just beginning strengths-based project team development. Unless otherwise indicated, these and other Gallup books can be purchased at www.gallupstrengthscenter.com or from other retailers.

Expanding Your Strengths, by Curt Liesveld, 2014. (Sold only in Kindle Edition through Amazon.)

Now Discover Your Strengths, by Donald Clifton and Marcus Buckingham, 2001.

The Power of 2, by Rodd Wagner and Gale Muller Wagner, 2009. (Importance of and eight key elements for powerful complementary partnerships, including strengths-based partnerships.)

Soar with Your Strengths, by Donald Clifton and Paul Nelson, 2010.

StrengthsFinder 2.0, by Tom Rath, 2007. (If you purchased your CliftonStrengths access code online, you may already have access to the digital copy of StrengthsFinder 2.0 at your CliftonStrengths login site— www.gallupstrengthscenter.com.)

Strengths Based Leadership, by Tom Rath and Barry Conchie, 2008. (See more about Strengths Based Leadership in the "CliftonStrengths Domain Resources" section.)


## Gallup Videos

There are many Gallup CliftonStrengths videos available to you. You can access free videos through Gallup's website, www.gallupstrengthscenter.com. You can also use a search engine to access Gallup videos by including key words, such as:

- Your Greatest Talents. (A short video explaining Gallup's strengths-based approach.)
- Gallup CliftonStrengths "Theme Thursdays."
  1. Presentations about each theme.
  2. In your search, next to "Theme Thursday," include the name of the theme that you want to learn about.
- Gallup CliftonStrengths [Talent Theme Name] (Short videos about each theme.)

## *CliftonStrengths Domains Resources*

Strengths Based Leadership, by Tom Rath and Barry Conchie, 2008.

- The Strengths Based Leadership book looks at the Clifton-Strengths Themes through the lens of leadership and the four CliftonStrengths Domains.
- Once you purchase the Strengths Based Leadership book, in the book you will find a CliftonStrengths assessment code.
  1. If you choose to take the assessment using the Strengths Based Leadership code, you will receive similar but different personalized CliftonStrengths reports as compared to StrengthsFinder 2.0.
  2. The Strengths Based Leadership's reports are written through the lens of leadership and the four CliftonStrengths Domains.
  3. Your personalized Strengths Based Leadership reports will include information about your top five themes' connection to the domains.
- If you have already taken the assessment through StrengthsFinder 2.0 but would like to also have the Strengths Based Leadership reports, you can use the Strengths Based Leadership book's online directions to use the book's code to acquire the reports.
  1. When prompted, indicate that you have already taken the CliftonStrengths assessment and follow the online prompts to get access to your Strengths Based Leadership reports.
  2. You will then be able to access your Strengths Based Leadership reports through your online CliftonStrengths account.

CliftonStrengths Coaching with Managers and Teams Kit (www.gallupstrengthscenter.com)

This kit will help you to dive deeper in understanding strengths-based team development and offers multiple exercises that you can use with your project team, including CliftonStrengths Domains exercises.

A team strengths grid template may be available at your Clifton-Strengths login site (www.gallupstrengthscenter.com).

*CliftonStrengths Coaching Resources (www.gallupstrengthscenter. com)*

CliftonStrengths Coaching Starter Kit
CliftonStrengths Coaching with Managers and Teams Kit

*Gallup-Certified Strengths Coach*

Some project managers enjoy leading and facilitating the initial strengths development processes for their project teams. However, some project managers prefer having some assistance in the initial stages of becoming a strengths-based project team. You have available to you Gallup-Certified Strengths Coaches who can work with you and your project team. If you are interested in learning more about and/or contacting a Gallup-Certified Strengths Coach, you can find more information about coaches at your CliftonStrengths login site (www.gallupstrengthscenter.com).

# Gallup, Inc. Research and Data (Online Resources)

Gallup Business Journal
Gallup Reports:

- The Clifton StrengthsFinder® 2.0 Technical Report (2014)
- State of the American Manager (2015)
- Re-engineering Performance Management (2017)
- State of the American Workplace (2017)

The resources and descriptions listed in Appendix A are current as of the book's publishing date.

# APPENDIX B

# Templates and Examples

Here are templates that you can use (and modify) to fit your needs. Each template is explained in its respective chapter. Also provided are completed examples for your reference.

## Chapter 2

Shared Expectations—Template and Prompts

| What are your expectations of me as the project manager? | What are my expectations of you as a team member? | As a team member of this group, what are your expectations of each other? |
|---|---|---|
| Start with: "Here is what you can expect from me as your Project Manager" | Start with: "What can I expect from you as an integral member of this team?" | Start with: "What are your expectations of each other as members of this team?" |
| | | |
| | | |
| | | |
| | | |
| | | |
| | | |
| | | |

Created (insert date) SIGNED: Project Manager _____

Team Member _____ Team Member _____

Team Member _____ Team Member _____

Team Member _____ Team Member _____

## Shared Expectations—Example

| What are your expectations of me as the project manager? | What are my expectations of you as a team member? | What are your expectations of each other as team members? |
|---|---|---|
| • I will start meetings on time<br>• I will end meetings on time<br>• I will distribute the agenda 48 hours in advance of meeting<br>• I will provide opportunities for our project team to become aware of our collective strengths<br>• I will encourage all team members to develop and use their strengths on the team | • I will complete my tasks on time<br>• I will reach out if I have questions<br>• I will utilize my talents and strengths toward the project<br>• I will articulate my talents, PM tool kit, and strengths that I bring to the team<br>• I will learn about and value the strengths of my fellow team members<br>• I will continue to develop my project management strengths | • We will reach out for help if needed<br>• We will resolve problems among ourselves<br>• We will support one another<br>• We will learn from each other<br>• We will engage in strengths conversations to further develop our strengths as a team<br>• We will value what each team member brings to the team<br>• We will apply our collective strengths as a team |

Created (insert date) SIGNED: Project Manager _____

Team Member _____ Team Member _____

Team Member _____ Team Member _____

Team Member _____ Team Member _____

# Chapter 4

Strengths Building Blocks Lists—Template

**STRENGTHS BUILDING BLOCKS LISTS**

| SPECIFIC TALENTS | SKILLS | KNOWLEDGE | EXPERIENCES | SPECIFIC STRENGTHS |
|---|---|---|---|---|

Strengths Building Blocks Lists—Example

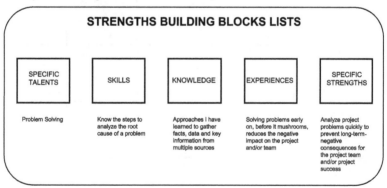

**STRENGTHS BUILDING BLOCKS LISTS**

| SPECIFIC TALENTS | SKILLS | KNOWLEDGE | EXPERIENCES | SPECIFIC STRENGTHS |
|---|---|---|---|---|
| Problem Solving | Know the steps to analyze the root cause of a problem | Approaches I have learned to gather facts, data and key information from multiple sources | Solving problems early on, before it mushrooms, reduces the negative impact on the project and/or team | Analyze project problems quickly to prevent long-term-negative consequences for the project team and/or project success |

Strengths Building Blocks Lists—Example for a Specific Strength

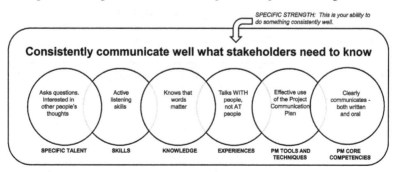

SPECIFIC STRENGTH: This is your ability to do something consistently well.

**Consistently communicate well what stakeholders need to know**

| Asks questions. Interested in other people's thoughts | Active listening skills | Knows that words matter | Talks WITH people, not AT people | Effective use of the Project Communication Plan | Clearly communicates - both written and oral |
|---|---|---|---|---|---|
| SPECIFIC TALENT | SKILLS | KNOWLEDGE | EXPERIENCES | PM TOOLS AND TECHNIQUES | PM CORE COMPETENCIES |

My Talents and Strengths Grid—Template

## My Talents and Strengths Grid

| Talent theme | Talent | + Investment: | Skills Experience Knowledge Practice | = Strength | Ways I use/ could use this specific strength |
|---|---|---|---|---|---|
|  | My specific talent | My specific talent investments | | My specific strength | |
|  |  |  | |  |  |
|  |  |  | |  |  |
|  |  |  | |  |  |
|  |  |  | |  |  |
|  |  |  | |  |  |

# Chapter 5

Process for Building/Developing a Talent—Template

| Talent Themes: |
|---|
| Specific Talent: |
| Investment: |
| Strength: |
| Ways to Use Strength on the Project Team: |

## Process for Building/Developing a Talent—Example

| |
|---|
| **Talent Themes:** Achiever®, Discipline®, and Harmony® |
| **Specific Talent:** Drive to get things done efficiently in a collaborative way |
| **Investment:** Demonstrate the benefits and value to find agreement among the project team to consistently use a Kanban board as a simple, step-by step tracking system |
| **Strength:** Equipping the project team to collaboratively and systematically keep track of what needs to get done and checking it off the project team's list |
| **Ways to Use Strength on the Project Team:** Collaboratively create action items assigned in project team meetings, post the action items in a place that is accessible to all project team members, communicate where the action items are posted, and then create a system for marking each action item complete |

# Chapter 6

## Project Team's Collective Strengths List—Example

| Team member | Specific strengths—consistent, proficient ability to: |
|---|---|
| Joe | Present complex project management topics to large groups |
| Susie | Connect people with people through email and social media to increase stakeholder engagement |
| Charles | Arrange details quickly staying attuned to the timing of the event and/or tasks |
| Allen | Interpret statistical data for others based on the individual's ability to understand statistical data |
| Sabrina | Mentor individuals toward their growth and development |
| Sally | Create compelling visuals (charts and diagrams) to quickly demonstrate project management concepts, tools, and techniques |

## Project Team Talent Theme Wall Chart—Example

| April | Joe | Mary | Sam | Tom |
|---|---|---|---|---|
| Activator | Achiever | Empathy | Achiever | Arranger |
| Arranger | Focus | Intellection | Ideation | Belief |
| Individualization | Harmony | Relator | Intellection | Individualization |
| Learner | Input | Responsibility | Learner | Relator |
| Relator | Maximizer | Strategic | Responsibility | Strategic |

*Source:* "CliftonStrengths Theme" names are registered marks of Gallup, Inc.

Project Team Leadership Domains Wall Chart—Example

|  | Executing leaders | Influencing leaders | Relationship building leaders | Strategic thinking leaders |
|---|---|---|---|---|
| April | Arranger | Activator | Individualization Relator | Learner |
| Joe | Achiever Focus | Maximizer | Harmony | Input |
| Mary | Responsibility |  | Empathy Relator | Intellection Strategic |
| Sam | Achiever Responsibility |  |  | Ideation Intellection Strategic |
| Tom | Arranger Belief |  | Individualization Relator | Strategic |

*Source:* "CliftonStrengths Theme" names are registered marks of Gallup, Inc.

Challenge Tracking: Applying your Project Team's Collective Strengths—Template

| Describe the challenge facing the project team | What collective strengths from the team did you apply? | What were the results? | What could have been done differently to improve those results? |
|---|---|---|---|
|  |  |  |  |
|  |  |  |  |
|  |  |  |  |

# Chapter 8

Professional Development Plan—Template

| Category | Organizational Knowledge | Functional Skills | Project Management | Strengths Development |
|---|---|---|---|---|
| Short-term goals (1 to 6 months) |  |  |  |  |
| Mid-term goals (6 months to 1 year) |  |  |  |  |
| Long-term goals (>1 year) |  |  |  |  |

# APPENDIX C

# Connecting Strengths and Project Management

## Strengths Themes as Used in Project Management*

*All theme names are trademarked by Gallup, Inc.

### Achiever®

You must accomplish something every day. You have great stamina and internal motivation. When you finish one task, you quickly want to work on another so you can complete milestones. You manage proactively by setting plans, working to achieve them, and asking people to report progress.

### Activator®

You want to make decisions and start quickly. Results of early actions will provide input into following decisions and actions. You want to be judged by your actions and results. You encourage others to action and help them overcome obstacles. You create a sense of urgency and energy when needed.

### Adaptability®

You live in the moment. Decisions made now create the future. You keep making progress in the face of unknowns. You balance conflicting demands of tasks and people, of various stakeholders, of risks, and of proposed changes. You understand reality, bring emotional stability, and do not need to control everything.

### Analytical®

You are objective, search for reasons, and want to see proof. You ask questions, research intensively, and then develop logical explanations. In ambiguous situations, you simplify concepts, recognize patterns, understand limits, describe causes and effects, and establish order. You fearlessly make honest decisions based upon facts.

### Arranger®

You are organized, yet flexible. You have defined values and priorities. You arrange people and other resources, improving work processes to best achieve your primary objectives. You thrive on cooperation and collaboration in complex settings. You depend on honest, timely, and transparent information to make rapid adjustments.

### Belief®

You possess enduring core values that guide and energize your behavior. You walk the talk as a dependable and trustworthy sounding board. You are committed to work and people, encouraging your team to display high ethics and to help others.

### Command®

You take charge, directly sharing your opinions and aligning people to your goals. You challenge others and lead forcefully when necessary. You thrive in crisis, making rapid decisions and encouraging others to take risks.

### Communication®

You speak and write clearly. You place high value on human interaction, talking with—not to—people. You tell stories to enliven your ideas, gain commitment, and maintain enthusiasm. You ask good questions, listen well, and help others express their feelings. You "think out loud" and encourage collaboration.

### Competition®

You want to outperform everyone either individually or as a team. This invigorates you and helps you achieve your ambitions. You define, measure, and ensure progress. You select contests you believe you can win and then celebrate your successes.

### Connectedness®

You believe everything happens for a reason and is part of something larger. Your thinking extends beyond your self-interests. You see no boundaries and celebrate when people find common ground around shared meaning. Your hopefulness helps you achieve personal and organizational goals.

### Consistency®

You treat everyone the same, with clear rules based upon values. You create a predictable and calm environment. You value loyalty and routines and accurately document requirements.

### Context®

You look back to understand the original purpose and past actions that shaped the present. You share stories to connect with people. You ask questions and take time to understand root causes. This perspective gives you confidence to decide what is enduring and what can change, inspiring confidence in followers.

### Deliberative®

You are a private person who identifies and analyzes risks, plans carefully, avoids problems, trusts your instincts, and makes no hasty decisions. You help others consider all factors in sensitive decisions. You have a few close friends in whom you confide. You only praise when it is well deserved.

## Developer®

You see potential and small improvements in people. You enjoy observing, advising, encouraging, challenging, and improving inexperienced people. You encourage teams to try, fail, and try again, helping them set appropriate expectations and celebrate success. By mentoring individuals, you develop effective teams.

## Discipline®

The world can be chaotic, but you create predictability with plans, priorities, routines, timelines, and structures. Through your attention to detailed planning and consistent execution, you create order and deliver effective and timely results. You carefully monitor progress, adhere to uncompromising standards, and celebrate excellence.

## Empathy®

You are highly instinctive and feel the emotions of others so strongly, it is as if they were your own. You do not necessarily agree with others' choices, but you understand. You respect everyone's feelings and help them express them. People trust your discretion and you help resolve conflict.

## Focus®

You work best when you know what is important and have a clear end goal. You define outcomes, determine priorities, set intermediate goals, follow through, make mid-course corrections, and deliver results. You concentrate deeply and are impatient with delays. You help others set goals and concentrate on critical issues.

## Futuristic®

You are intrigued by the future and enjoy describing your conceptions of it. Your emotional yet realistic contemplations help others to understand how supporting your project helps them accomplish their goals.

### Harmony®

You look for a common ground to find agreement. You value expert perspectives, perhaps merging ideas as long as you retain your basic values and shared sense of purpose. You have a calm, facilitating manner, avoid confrontation, bring practical knowledge, and strive for consensus.

### Ideation®

You are energized by finding new perspectives on familiar situations. You are innovative and creative, love to brainstorm, and strive to make things better. You take calculated risks and share excitement. You create useful plans, overcoming resource limits and risks.

### Includer®

You feel the pain of those who are left out and understand the power of a larger team of active and unified participants in which all voices are heard. You are accepting, as you feel we are all equally important. You ensure information and decision making are widely shared.

### Individualization®

You perceive differences in how people think, feel, and behave. You bring out the best in each person and foster effective, diverse teams in which everyone is encouraged to do what they do best. As a mentor and leader, you treat each person according to their unique needs and dreams.

### Input®

Your curiosity enables you to be a great researcher. You enjoy being up to date and gathering and sharing information. You view whatever you collect—ideas or tangible items—as resources. You may be an expert or good at making concepts seem real.

## Intellection®

You enjoy taking quiet time to read and think. While your thoughts may be focused or diverse, you often generate wisdom and clarity. You help your team make better decisions by asking great questions, giving your honest opinions, and engaging in deep conversations.

## Learner®

You are energized by the process of learning and considering possibilities. You excel on short project assignments and as a change agent where you need to learn quickly. As you continuously study and improve, you gain confidence. You help your team improve by co-learning with them and tracking lessons learned.

## Maximizer®

Your greatest joy is taking good performance of your own, of another individual, or of a team to a higher level. You prefer to capitalize upon raw talent. You strive for quality and excellence.

## Positivity®

You always see and communicate the good. You lift others with your enthusiasm. Life and work are fun. You give people frequent praise and focus on making progress no matter the situation. Your hope for the future, good humor, and eagerness to celebrate make you a valued team member.

## Relator®

You enjoy being around your close friends, learning about their feelings and goals. You derive satisfaction from working hard with these friends. You honor trust and show respect.

### Responsibility®

You enjoy volunteering, and when you commit, no one needs to check your progress. You have the highest ethics, usually fulfilling your many obligations, and making amends when you cannot. You are a serious, dedicated role model. You may feel overwhelmed, but you are satisfied when you complete commitments.

### Restorative™

You diagnose problems, determine root causes, and implement solutions. Bad news with no sugar coating motivates you, whether it concerns people or things. You can identify risks and devise contingency plans in advance.

### Self-Assurance®

Your confidence inspires others. You research issues and listen to experts, but then make up your own mind and act decisively. You completely commit to critical challenges not because you have no fear, but because you know someone needs to lead and you are bold and resolute.

### Significance®

You want to make a lasting difference in this world and be known for it. You dream big dreams, need affirmation, fear failure, but are comfortable with risk and public scrutiny. You champion others' needs and achievements. You want to associate with other top performers.

### Strategic®

You plan backward from goals to various means of accomplishing them. You see patterns where others see chaos. You research alternatives and select one—often avoiding potential problems. You see the big picture and are flexible concerning how to achieve it.

## Woo®

You enjoy meeting new people and discovering common interests or other connections. The thrill of meeting a new person may be greater than developing a deep relationship. You naturally put people at ease and facilitate interchange of ideas. You ask questions and get others to support your goals.

*Source:* From Kloppenborg. *Contemporary Project Management,* 3E. © 2015 South-Western, a part of Cengage, Inc. Reproduced by permission.
www.cengage.com/permissions

# APPENDIX D

# Strengths Conversational Prompts for Project Teams

Strengths conversations are instrumental for cultivating and sustaining your project team's strengths-based talent development culture. When you engage others in strengths conversations, you are helping them to articulate their talents and develop their strengths. Strengths conversations will also help you to develop strengths-based complementary partnerships and maximize and leverage the collective strengths of your project team.

Strengths conversations include asking **specific questions** about a person's talents and strengths *and* **active listening**. A list of strengths-based conversational prompts and ideas are listed as follows to help you and your project team members begin engaging in strengths conversations. Also consider adding "active listening skills" into your PM tool kit to better equip you to fully engage in strengths conversations.

**Suggested Questions:**

|  | |
|--|--|
| | "What did you initially think about your *Signature Themes Report?*" |
| | "Do you think the summaries of your top five dominant talent themes describe you? Tell me more…" |
| | "Tell me about your **specific talents** from your _____ talent theme." If the person is not sure how to answer this prompt, have them pull out their *Signature Themes Report* and talk about the words and phrases in their theme summaries that they highlighted. |
| | "What do you like about your talents?" |
| | "What is challenging about your talents?" |
| | "Did you see yourself using talents from your _____ talent theme today? In what ways?" |
| | "What specific talents from your _____ talent theme are you most excited about? Tell me more…" |

| | |
|---|---|
| | "What are some examples of how you use your specific talents from your _____talent theme (at work, home, volunteering, etc.)?" |
| | "What specific talents have you discovered from knowing about your dominant _____ talent theme? Besides knowing about your dominant talent theme, how did you discover these specific talents you just identified?" |
| | Find someone that shares a talent theme with you and compare notes. After your conversation, what specific talent similarities and differences did you notice? |
| | "A **strength** is the ability to do something consistently, very well.<br>• Tell me about one of your strengths.<br>• Which of your dominant talent themes describes talents that might be a foundation for the strength you named?<br>• Articulate more of your strengths." |
| | "Think of an example of a challenging problem that you have solved on your own. What role did your talents and/or talent themes play in your approach to the problem? How did you use your strengths to solve the problem?" |
| | "Think about the times you have felt extremely proud of a workplace achievement. How did you use your strengths to be successful in one or more of those situations?" |
| | "How have you used your specific talents and strengths on a project team (your current team or a previous team)?" |
| | "What project management tools or techniques have you invested in your talents? What specific project management strengths have you developed from that investment?" |
| | "In what ways do/could some of your specific talents from your _____ talent theme help you when working with project team members to achieve a common goal?" |
| | "How specifically can you use your talents/strengths to help our/your project team build relationships?" |
| | "How specifically can you use your talents/strengths to motivate our/your project team?" |
| | "How specifically can you use your talents/strengths to help our/your project team think through approaches to team challenges and make good decisions?" |
| | "How specifically can you use your talents/strengths to help our/your project team get things done?" |
| | "In what specific ways to do you currently/potentially see our/your project team using the project team members' collective strengths as a team?" |

# Index

## OTHER TITLES IN OUR PORTFOLIO AND PROJECT MANAGEMENT COLLECTION

Timothy J. Kloppenborg, Editor

- *Project Management and Leadership Challenges, Volume I: Applying Project Management Principles for Organizational Transformation* by Mirza, M. Aslam
- *Innoliteracy: From Design Thinking to Tangible Change* by Valade-Amland, Steinar
- *Project Management and Leadership Challenges, Volume III: Respecting Diversity, Building Team Meaningfulness, and Growing Into Leadership Roles* by Mirza, M. Aslam
- *Project Management and Leadership Challenges, Volume II: Understanding Human Factors And Workplace Environment* by Mirza, M. Aslam
- *Why Projects Fail: Nine Laws for Success* by Tony Martyr

## Announcing the Business Expert Press Digital Library

*Concise e-books business students need for classroom and research*

This book can also be purchased in an e-book collection by your library as

- a one-time purchase,
- that is owned forever,
- allows for simultaneous readers,
- has no restrictions on printing, and
- can be downloaded as PDFs from within the library community.

Our digital library collections are a great solution to beat the rising cost of textbooks. E-books can be loaded into their course management systems or onto students' e-book readers. The **Business Expert Press** digital libraries are very affordable, with no obligation to buy in future years. For more information, please visit **www.businessexpertpress.com/librarians**. To set up a trial in the United States, please email **sales@businessexpertpress.com**.

CPSIA information can be obtained
at www.ICGtesting.com
Printed in the USA
BVHW061245190919
558906BV00006B/164/P

9 781947 843417